brilliant
future

future
brilliant

Work out what you want and
plan how to get there

Chris Sangster

Prentice Hall

an imprint of Pearson Education

London • New York • San Francisco • Toronto • Sydney • Tokyo • Singapore
Hong Kong • Cape Town • Madrid • Paris • Milan • Munich • Amsterdam

PEARSON EDUCATION LIMITED

Head Office:
Edinburgh Gate
Harlow CM20 2JE
Tel: +44 (0)1279 623623
Fax: +44 (0)1279 431059

London Office:
128 Long Acre
London WC2E 9AN
Tel: +44 (0)20 7447 2000
Fax: +44(0)20 7240 5771

Website: www.business-minds.com

First published in Great Britain 2002

© Pearson Education Limited 2002

The right of Chris Sangster to be identified as author of this work has been asserted by
him in accordance with the Copyright, Designs and Patents Act 1988.

ISBN 0 273 65601 5

British Library Cataloguing in Publication Data
A catalogue record for this book is available from the British Library.

All rights reserved; no part of this publication may be reproduced, stored in a retrieval
system, or transmitted in any form or by any means, electronic, mechanical,
photocopying, recording, or otherwise without either the prior written permission of the
Publishers or a licence permitting restricted copying in the United Kingdom issued by the
Copyright Licensing Agency Ltd, 90 Tottenham Court Road, London WlP OLP. This book
may not be lent, resold, hired out or otherwise disposed of by way of trade in any form of
binding or cover other than that in which it is published, without the prior consent of the
Publishers.

10 9 8 7 6 5 4 3 2

Designed by Claire Brodmann Book Designs, Lichfield, Staffs.
Typeset by Northern Phototypesetting Co. Ltd, Bolton
Printed and bound in Great Britain by Biddles Ltd, Guildford & King's Lynn

The Publishers' policy is to use paper manufactured from sustainable forests.

To Kay & Ross
Yours is the future

Contents

part one

get personal

In this section you will take a close look at yourself – a very close look. Try to see yourself as others do (the good as well as the 'less good' bits!) And when you've done that you're ready to start looking towards the development path you'd really like to take.

1 Here's lookin' at you

A brilliant future, your Brilliant Future. Sounds good doesn't it? So how can you go about achieving one? Well, here is a good place to start. This book will help you design the route map to guide you through all the decisions, options and possibilities life throws at you. Taking you through step-by-step using a series of exercises, checklists and questionnaires you can identify your strengths and weakness, likes and dislikes, so that you know what you need to do. From motivating yourself, to getting where you want to be – and assessing as you go – *Brilliant Future* will help you work smarter, get focused and move forward.

So, here you are poised at the crossroads. The signs give you the options. At least you've noticed them – and are reviewing them – this time round. You may well have passed through many of the previous junctions without pausing – eye fixed unwavering on that distant goal. Missed opportunities and linear progression, potentially experiencing tiresome frustrations.

When you wake up on a work morning, does any of that youthful 'whoopee' feeling remain? If not – why not? Can you look back on elements of your life to date and relive the enjoyment you experienced then? Projecting forward, can you see exciting times ahead – or is life getting a bit predictable? If you do see positive light in your tunnel, as well as at the end of it, how can you get this light to burn more brightly?

Personal planning is largely about empowerment – about taking charge of your life and how it develops.

It's about:

■ knowing the rules and policies so that you can flex them to their legal extremes

- holding your finger on the pulse of progress – your progress and the progress of others – to make sure that opportunities are gained, not lost

- keeping aware of how things are developing and responding flexibly

- working together co-operatively, not by grinding everyone else into the ground.

We'll be looking at assertiveness within the belonging–co-operative sequence later. For now think of a rock climber reaching the peak, working in conjunction with others; not using the heads of colleagues as stepping stones to the top.

You'll find lots of sections where you're asked to respond in some way. These will help you:

- find out
- work out
- chill out.

You will be *finding out* by answering questionnaires; *working out* by responding to exercises, short case studies, etc and *chilling out* through 'thinking time reflections'.

Don't just scan through them, thinking – 'Oh yeah, that's a nice idea; that might be something to think about – later'. Think about it now – and write down your thoughts so that you can cross reference them later when we're looking at a planning system – the *ID Plan*. If you use a notebook make a note of the related book page number alongside, so that you don't waste time during review trying to figure out the context.

Who are you?

Spend a moment finding out about yourself. You can use either the space provided or a notebook to jot down your ideas.

Find out time-1

Make some notes about your immediate thoughts on the following:

■ What do you really enjoy doing?

_____

■ Overwhelming financial commitments aside, what would you do with your life?

_____

■ If you're working just now, which element of your job do you like best?

_____

■ Is your present job the best way to develop this further?

_____

■ If so, how can you increase its priority in your work responsibilities?

_____

■ Is there a hobby or interest outside work, which you'd love to develop further?

_____

■ Is your daily commuting commitment an acceptable use of your time?

_____

- Do you feel a buzz when you're working on a project with others?

- What can you do to make this buzz expand to 'whoopee' proportions?

- What are the five key items on your 'shopping list for Life'?

Opportunities for personal development

You may have come across the phrases 'lifelong learning' or 'continuing professional development' at work. There are lots of ways to progress your development through workplace learning opportunities provided you're actually working in a workplace, of course! Grab the opportunities where you spot them. Don't rely on Human Resource (HR) Departments though – they have limited resources, imagination and enthusiasm, so don't hang about waiting for them to plan your life. Do it yourself.

If you've been on training courses and sat during a session thinking 'this is not really relevant for me' or, worse still, 'I already know all this'? then the idea of more courses may not appeal. But it is possible to select a course (or other learning event) which does actually match your needs. What do you need to know to do that? You have to know what your needs are – in detail, not in vague 'have a better awareness of the key concepts' terms. That's just waffle – don't settle for it.

We'll look at the benefits of writing and thinking objectively so that you can:

- match your needs with learning outcomes (or results)
- kick up a fuss if the course content doesn't match up to the provider's promise
- get involved in the process yourself
- figure out what you need, in specific terms
- select the ways you prefer to learn things
- check how effective the learning was afterwards
- make sure you go on a course where its objectives match your needs.

But remember, if you've selected a course, which meets its objectives but doesn't satisfy yours, (when you think about it during and after the course), don't then feel that it's the course which is not right – it's perhaps more a case of your choice lacking depth. Empowerment equals personal responsibility. Courses aren't the only way of learning – we'll look at some of the other options as we move along the development path.

The 'path' of personal development

Talking about paths, think of your personal development as the winding path which you choose to take as you move along a wide track. The outer boundaries of this track contain all the rules, policies and potential experiences which are options open to us all. Your path is the journey that you choose to take along that track.

We started at a sign-posted junction. At each point along the track, there are similar options open. Sometimes we choose to change, divert, or even double back slightly. Sometimes, we choose to move on down the track, following milestones. It's your choice – it's you that's empowered to establish your path.

Others will be moving forward by following their own, similarly-selected paths. Sometimes these will cross; sometimes run parallel; sometimes perhaps block your path for a while. Some paths will progress faster than yours; some slower – each is a unique way of travelling along the track, because each one of us is unique. But the track is there, full of opportunities, if you keep your eyes and mind open.

Chill out time-1

Check through these previous sentences again and try to picture what is being represented.

It might help to draw a quick sketch. Imagine the outer limits of the track and a winding line as your own development path.

Think of a few milestones along the way, which you could use to check your progress.

Think how other people's winding lines could affect your own.

Work/life balance

Do you have the time to focus on your own development? You must have. Is society really as busy as it pretends to be nowadays? We're told we've:

- ■ no time to shop – get it on the internet
- ■ no time to date – get a virtual partner instead

- no time to talk – hide behind your voicemail but then waste your time trying to penetrate someone else's voicemail

- no time to discuss things face-to-face, send e-mails instead

- no time to have a home life as you're too busy scoring points at your desk until the boss finally leaves.

Where's it all leading? Should we be standing on our heads trying to manage time and stress – or should we be probing at the origins? Are overworked executives just working long or would they be better working smart? Why are companies proud of the fact that their people work the longest hours in Europe? 'People are our greatest asset' – but the company's possibly into asset management and 'bottom line value added' as well – when does an asset become a mere statistic?

You can progress in work; you can progress outside work. Frustrations in one sometimes focus development in the other. We are aiming for some equilibrium point. It's called a 'work/life balance' nowadays. It often equates with someone desperately trying to cut back on a massive time commitment at work to allow them to recognize their kids or partner at the weekend.

There's a lot of change around, not all of it thought through and not all of it beneficial. Note your responses to the following.

Work out time-1

1 'Jobs for life are a thing of the past' – how do you feel about this statement?

2 State three benefits of the fixed term contract.

3 State three disadvantages of the fixed term contract.

4   What are the main ways of motivating a staff member on a fixed term contract?

5   Given the open-ended opportunity, what actions would you take to improve your present work/life balance?

6   Can you achieve any of these? If not, what is blocking you?

There may be both benefits and disadvantages, but ultimately this situation will alter people's expectations of employment. Short-term job security can encourage a higher level of self-empowerment – if you don't look to your brilliant future, who else will? When looking at your own empowerment, you need to be looking at the widest scope possible.

- Is it a big deal moving house?
- Would it really ruin the kids' education changing school?
- Is it really out of the question to retrain or focus on developing a newly-discovered skill further?
- Would it be possible to job share, to free you to try alternatives?
- Is self-employment an option – but if you think it is, have you thought through a proper business plan, with your eyes wide open?
- Is early retirement going to seem as attractive several years down the line, unless you can find outlets for your latent skills?

The opportunities are there – empowerment helps you grasp them and apply them effectively.

The bigger picture

How do we keep a focus on 'the bigger picture', or perhaps, how do we first see what the bigger picture is?

- By stepping back and looking up – looking at the birds in the sky rather than the cracks in the pavement.

- By focusing on the 'Now' and the 'Future' and not getting bogged down in the past.

- By being aware of what is going on in the world, away from our immediate doorstep – and learning lessons where they apply.

- By becoming aware of the broader implications of some of our potential actions – and how they relate to the actions and lives of others.

Do you, for example, continue to accept the fact that you might get a place on the next training course in seven months' time, or do you do a bit of research and find an open learning programme which is more relevant, more flexible and available now? A small change to the current status quo, perhaps, but what happens if others follow your lead, the Training Department warms to the idea and improves its policy, the production company is motivated to produce additional open learning programmes, which are then marketed internationally – the picture gets bigger.

Think holistically

Another part of this big picture is thinking in a holistic way. You may have heard the word used in relation to health. It basically means that the overall effect is worth more than the sum of the individual parts – take care of yourself in a variety of ways and the outcome will be a person who is healthy overall, in mind as well as body. It works well for the spirit or soul as well.

In the same way, apply a variety of skills and knowledge in your work (some of which you may have learned in the 'University of Life') and your overall work competence and professionalism will become greater. The reverse is obviously true – which is why it is often valuable having people on local community or sports committees who can apply business ideas to make them run a little more efficiently.

This type of thinking works well in team activities too, as we'll see. Take a group of individuals, each with a particular skill, and combine these skills together. The team's final effort will be better than the result which any one of these individuals could have accomplished. As well as this improved achievement, we have a bunch of motivated individuals who have managed to excel in an activity which they probably wouldn't have had the confidence to try as solo participants. That's certainly the view if you're thinking co-operatively.

If you're thinking assertively, you might consider it a drawback that each (or one) of the individuals hasn't managed to win. Just remember, in negotiation nowadays, we're going for win/win outcomes. Our approach here is that assertiveness is a step along the way to ultimate co-operation.

Co-operative thinking has a part to play in facing up to stress as well. Accepting that some of the causes of stress are only going to be reduced gradually, we still have to combat stress in the short term. Planning helps – it helps more where someone doesn't come along at the eleventh hour and ruin your plans with additional rush jobs or a dramatic change of mind.

Learn to say 'No' politely. Feel in control and you're less likely to finish up dreading going to work. Time management, good communication, effective project planning all help. Learn how to switch off. Senior executives power nap (although sleeping on the job tends to be cause for instant dismissal for more lowly staff – figure out ways to do it less noticeably). Combine these various skills together and the (holistic) outcome gives greater control in a stressful environment.

Summary

So, let's see where we've got to:

■ we focus the mind

■ we relax the body

■ we think as openly as possible

■ we identify our skills

■ we log the areas which need improvement.

With a limited number of these key shortfall areas, we may look for ways of compensating (on the basis that we can't be good at doing everything!) If you're a star at 'x', you can afford to say 'I don't do "y" – ask someone else'. The number of 'don't dos' must be limited, however, or you're on shaky ground, however much of a star you are.

Then what?

■ We record activities and outcomes which we have completed.

■ We identify areas which need further action.

■ We create written plans for future development which allow us to map the way forward.

Although we don't always learn in a linear way, it makes sense to learn the principles we hope to apply before we try applying them. Crawl before you walk before you run before you fly. Otherwise, you're learning by trial and error – character-building, perhaps, but not time-effective. And time, as we're always told nowadays, is money.

Planning your brilliant future involves you in:

■ analysing your own strengths and shortfalls

■ figuring out the development learning you need

■ being aware of the range of options open to you

■ doing things in the way you prefer to do them

- keeping an eye on the 'bigger picture'
- thinking objectively and logically
- mapping details in some form of written plan
- being involved in team as well as individual activities
- keeping an open and flexible attitude to change
- reviewing progress and priorities regularly.

Let's get down to business.

2 Where am I now?

So far, you've taken a few sidelong glances at yourself in the mirror: am I doing what I want to do; is this really what my future offers me; what improvements will I really have to make?

Now's the time to step back from the mirror and get a wider picture – to review where you stand at the moment in some detail. Not just 'off the top of the head' stuff – this really does need writing down so that you can see how it progresses. Once we've played around with ideas a little, we'll start using the organized planning system, *ID Plan*, which links with this book.

Sheep and goats

Although the possible paths are almost limitless, there are perhaps two options right at the beginning.

- Are you working fairly conventionally? or
- Are you self-employed, working as an associate or whatever?

Are you a company employee, able to call on the resources of the training department, financed courses, work-based opportunities to learn (and reinforce learning) and the other positive benefits of being 'in the system'? Or are you outside the conventional system, as self-employed, under-employed or unemployed, where there are different (but not necessarily fewer) opportunities around?

For easy reference, let's refer to them as:

- *sheep* – if you're working within a company structure; *and*
- *goats* – if you're working less conventionally.

No deep implications intended – don't bother looking for them. Some people think sheep are stupid – not so, if you take the time to study their funny little ways. Sure, when threatened, they opt for flight rather than fight and stick together in groups for moral support – is that so stupid?

Goats, on the other hand, are more independent thinkers who will cross any imposed boundary if given half an opportunity. They'll grab anything that's available, as well. Self-employed entrepreneurs, to a 'T'!

So, first question … are you a sheep or a goat at heart?

Find out time-2

Circle your preferred choice for each of these pairs.

1A I prefer a regular working day with my evenings and weekend relatively to myself.

B I prefer working long hours some days with little or nothing happening on other days.

2A I prefer to know exactly how much and when my pay cheque will arrive each month.

B I prefer to earn a monthly sum which is directly related to the amount of work I do.

3A I prefer to have a company infrastructure which I am part of (to some degree).

B I prefer to do my own 'leg work' to gain support, funding, information, etc.

4A   I prefer to rely on others to provide my daily workload.

B   I prefer to have to approach potential clients to set up my own contracts, etc.

5A   I prefer to have the social benefits of a group of work colleagues.

B   I prefer feeling more a 'temp' outsider, even when working within a client company.

6A   I prefer having informal technical and knowledge backup to call on to maintain progress.

B   I prefer having to figure things out for myself or find my own reference sources.

7A   I prefer having ready access to resources, office equipment, etc.

B   I prefer providing my own facilities – or hiring/borrowing them.

8A   I prefer working within a hierarchy, with most of my dealings directly above or below.

B   I prefer dealing with all levels, as well as clients, suppliers and officialdom.

9A   I prefer working in a relatively ordered and predictable environment.

B   I prefer living more on my nerves, on a day-to-day basis.

It's no great secret – the 'A' statements tend towards *sheep* thinking, while the 'B' statements are more *goat* thinking.

But it goes deeper than that. If you've started by placing yourself in one or other pigeon-hole and automatically selected all the 'A's or all the 'B's – give these questions a second, deeper thought. Perhaps you prefer some of the benefits of working within a company infrastructure (3A, 6A and 7A, for example) but you also hunger for more freedom and flexibility (as with 1B, 3B and 4B). In other words, you might be working within – and enjoying the majority of – a sheep environment just now but also have goat tendencies. Or vice versa.

Take Dave as an example, for a moment. He's self-employed – has been for years – with all the associated joys and troubles. The 15+ years before that, he worked for a variety of financial institutions, with varying degrees of autonomy so he has both sheep and goat tendencies, with a bias towards the goat now. He enjoys the freedom and responsibility side of self-employment – but is uncomfortable with the cold calling and fluctuating income. While company-employed, he liked the way that tedious issues like pensions and legislation were organized for him – but disagreed on many occasions with the decisions and politics coming from senior managers.

I guess we all think something like that. The human being is a complex animal – with the majority having elements of both sheep and goat. The questions you might want to address are whether you are a goat trapped in a sheep flock (or vice versa) and how can you improve your situation to get that whoopee factor going again?

So, some of what follows will apply to all, some is more sheep orientated, and some will be more for goat-thinkers. Where I think it's relevant, I'll indicate which.

Finding your position

Find out time-3

Here are some questions to ask yourself, to establish where you are on your personal development path. We touched on one or two in the first chapter – think of them as practice. This is for real – the rest of your life depends on it! Note your responses to these, you'll be referring to them in the future. Some might change in time – that's part of development as well.

1   List your five key skills.

2   When with other people, what are you happiest doing?

_____

3   Which 'sheep' attribute (if any) do you think would be most valuable to your
     way of life?

_____

4   Which 'goat' attribute (if any) do you think would be most valuable to your
     way of life?

_____

5   Do you work best on your own or as part of a team?

_____

6   What would you really like to be doing, one year from now?

_____

7   List, in order, the three things that really motivate you.

_____

8   If you could change two things in the way you're running your life just now,
     what would they be?

_____

9 What's your main worry in life, which may impede your progress periodically?

---

10 Which single skill would you most like to excel in, which you currently don't?

There's quite a lot of real truths in there, if you have given your answers a bit of thought. It might be worthwhile going over them again and expanding on one or two, just to check that you've got to the heart of the matter.

Very few of us are doing what we want to do all of the time. By knowing ourselves – really knowing what we desire, dislike and dismiss – we are more likely to reach that goal of doing what we want all the time by making the path as direct as possible, with limited detours and no retracing of our steps.

Work out time-2

Consider the answers you have given to the FIND OUT questionnaire on page 5.

With a coloured or highlighter pen, mark any response which surprises you in any way – maybe because it's not the answer you would have expected yourself to make; or you didn't realize you felt strongly on that issue; or perhaps because it's showing a glimmer of a real you which you have been keeping submerged. Whatever it is – it's giving you a deeper insight about your real feelings and priorities.

So, let's say you've managed to find at least three things that surprise you about yourself. Think about them for a while and consider the implications.

You know yourself better than anyone else – your likes, dislikes, dreams, desires, the list's endless. You obviously know your current activities and priorities.

Think about those surprises that you've highlighted.

Take some simple examples, to give you the idea:
- I might have established that I actually like producing short reports. I never have the time to do them properly – and I'm invariably interrupted, spoiling my flow. But I enjoy seeing the results. So – how can I get more involved in writing?
- Let's say I am on several committees and find I work best when there is a proposal on the table to discuss and amend, rather than people going round and round in circles with unrelated suggestions. How can I adapt this to perform better at meetings?
- I may have established that my main frustration is the slow pace of progress in my department – and difficulty at accepting imposed priorities. Do I have enough experience and confidence to try to change department or job … or go out on my own?

Focusing on your current situation, what can you do in the next month to make some element(s) of these surprise issues change your life in some way?

Note down thoughts while you remember them.

So far, so good. You've identified one or two focus points for development in the next month or so. All good positive stuff.

What blocks your progress?

Still thinking positively – but realistically – what are some of your blocks? The kinds of things that stand in your way; take up your time unproductively; prevent your path from progressing along a particular direction. We all have them – it's what we do about them that's the important issue.

Although there are obvious overlaps and parallels, sheep blocks can be different from goat blocks. A boss who keeps coming up with last-minute things to do, upsetting your planned workload, is a sheep block. Clients can do similar things to a goat ... but the goat has greater potential to respond through charging extra 'rush/emergency' fees.

A goat block could be the long-drawn-out tendering processes which are demanded nowadays, to allow so-called 'transparency'. Very time-consuming – and frustrating on the occasions when you see them stealing your ideas and doing the job internally! The more that people are working together co-operatively, the fewer the blocks there should be ... but we're talking long-term goal here.

How about your personal blocks?

Find out time-4

To establish your key blocks and possible strategies, consider the following and write down your responses.

1   Make a list of several things which you currently have pending, still to complete.

2 Against each, note the major block which is preventing it happening. (It doesn't have to be an external factor – YOU might be creating the block yourself, in some way.)

3A Sheep – write down three key blocks which impede your progress at work.

3B Goats – write down three key blocks which slow down your business progress.

4 Identify two or more skills/knowledge areas which you think you should be more competent at, in order to progress your life more effectively.

5 Identify one or more skill/knowledge area(s) at which others think you should be more capable – but which you feel would be very difficult for you to improve. Make sure that you write it down.

Have a short break.

Work out time-3

Consider the area or areas that you have just noted in 4 and 5 above.

On a scale of 1–10 (where 10 is very important), how important is each area to your future progress in life, your job or self-development?

When you have done that – consider your responses.

Where you have scored it 5 or above – you'll have to take steps to improve these core skills.

Where you have a 4 or less – is it worth bothering about?

For the low-scoring one(s), think of a strategy that you could use to get out of doing that particular activity – (we considered this earlier, where you were a star at something else). If you are working as a team member, perhaps someone else is good at this particular activity. Make notes, to help clarify your ideas.

So, you're clearer about your key skills, the areas you need to develop further and the blocks which are standing in your way. And you've thought of strategies to progress things further.

Now, you can see the direction you're taking – and you're clearer in your mind as to whether this is the best route. Don't be afraid of what you've written. Sometimes it's the immediate thought that's the true one.

Chill out time-2

What's your immediate response if I ask you:

'What do you really want to do with your life?'

- Lead travel groups …
- Write …
- Be a consultant …
- Do exactly what I'm doing now …
- Run a farm …
- Be a commercially-successful painter …
- Have a greater decision-making role …

The list is endless. But the real answer's in there, if you think about it. Do.

Be patient, but persevere

If you want to do something badly enough, you will make it happen. *You can* influence the direction and pace of your own path. Don't just settle back thinking 'if it was meant to happen, it will happen some time … there's nothing I can do to influence things' – you can – and it's important to acknowledge that you have this control. However, things do take time to happen, even with your input. I designed the original ID Plan system that goes with this book over 15 years ago, but 'lifelong learning' and 'continuing professional development' hadn't been thought of in the mid-1980s – so there was little demand for personal planning. The time was not then – it is now.

This can be the hardest thing to accept – the time element. We tend to think very much in the 'Now'. Thirty or so years ago, hire purchase was the major method of purchasing higher cost items. There was, however, a bit of a stigma attached. Many people would try to save up for something like a TV or new sofa, rather than get involved in HP. Nowadays, we use the credit card and sort out the repayment later. We get what we want now – and allow the future reckoning to sort itself out.

In personal planning, we must live with the fact that we won't always get what we want, when we want it. However, if we can define our goal precisely, the majority of us can keep our eyes firmly on that milestone up ahead. Sure, our path might meander – but we'll ultimately get there. Getting round the various blocks may refine and amend our original goal – but that's OK – the outcome may even be improved as a result.

A sign on a car read:

'Employ a teenager – while they know everything!

It's very frustrating, when young, to feel that you are capable of doing more that the mundane tasks you're often given. You make suggestions – but nothing changes. You have sharp ideas – but the old manager won't do anything about it.

It can be exactly the same when you're older and the managers are younger! There seems to be something which happens to people when they get to more senior positions – be it manager, politician or (even) parent. They become part of the system – become conventional, have to watch their backs – and, nowadays, get caught up in the spin.

It's part of what's called the 'tall poppy effect'. Anyone who sticks their head too high above the field is in danger of getting it cut off – to permit the status quo to return. There are always the politics of the situation (with a small 'p') – sometimes, the reasons will be valid; sometimes, there are background arguments (or as-yet secret plans for the future) about which we mere proles may not be aware but which will influence current and future decisions. Hang on in there, though – if your idea is a good one, its time will come.

Learn to be a smart tall poppy – bend in the wind so that your head remains at around the same height ... for the moment. You're no longer a threat – but ready to bob back up with your ideas again, when the wind's blowing in the right direction! Think in the long term when you need to – store your ideas, ready to be aired again when the time is appropriate. But never lose that conviction that these ideas are good.

Some people retain this long-term faith in themselves by making affirmations – it's basically telling yourself (out loud – while looking at yourself in the mirror, if that helps) that you will succeed, in as specific terms as possible.

Chill out time-3

Find a quiet space and focus on your own thoughts for a moment.

Think of a good idea which would make your life better/easier/happier.

Picture the surroundings which are necessary for it to happen.

Store the thought in your mind – or even jot it down.

_____

_____

_____

_____

_____

Some day – when the time is right – you will make it happen!

Foundations for the future are built on past experience

Back to the present now.

We're building the foundations for your personal planning here. Foundations don't have to be massive – but they need to be strong and carefully thought through. Whatever age you are, you're standing at a threshold. Ahead of you – the future and all those potential ideas which still have to reach fruition.

Behind you – the experience you have had to date. Some good; some dynamic; some positive and needing further development; some indicating areas which you will definitely wish to bypass next time they appear.

As your journey progresses, priorities change. Think of your first CV and some of the things you included as relevant experience – pretty embarassing now, perhaps? If your path is progressing, new experiences will build on previous experiences – or selected elements. Your preferred future direction should become more apparent when you review your path to date.

Find out time-5

Consider the following, making notes in your book.

1   Think of a situation where you were really proud of the outcome. Describe the situation.

---

2   List the life and work activities you find really stimulating.

---

3 Which activity would you be happiest doing right now, given the chance?

_____

4 Do you have an interest or hobby which you could incorporate into your working life?

_____

5 How would you maintain your enthusiasm if you were applying your hobby as a job?

Chill out time-4

You've covered a lot in this chapter with lots noted down for further consideration.

You should have a clearer idea of who you are, including your:

- strengths
- experiences
- priorities
- preferences
- sheep or goat tendencies
- future direction.

Spend a little time going back through what you've written, in order to get a broader picture of where you stand at the moment and an indication of the direction your path will take.

Consider some of the implications.

Summary

So, through these various exercises, you've now focused in some detail on how you currently stand – with a view of the key issues that govern your life. You've got a bigger picture of exactly where and how you stand at the moment.

We'll be checking back on it periodically, as we progress along the path. Not in a negative way – no 'blame and shame'; no 'if only ...'. The past is something we learn from and move on from positively. But the past gives us the foundations and experience – which help us see more clearly down our individual development path.

3 Strengths and shortfalls

We've already touched briefly on this – now's the time to bite the bullet. We're into positive thinking, so notice – we're talking 'shortfalls' – not weaknesses, failures or whatever. You can't be perfect at everything and there are always new things to learn, so there will always be shortfall areas. It's what we do about them that's important! On the plus side, of course, there are your many and varied strengths.

Work out time-4

Think of somebody – your boss, partner, a close friend, somebody that you know well. Really focus on them for the next few minutes.

1 List a maximum of five of his or her shortfall areas – things that you would expect him or her to be able to do more effectively. Leave a space alongside each, for your additional ideas.

2 Against each shortfall, write ideas of what he/she could do to improve capabilities.

3 For the same individual, note down several of his or her strengths. It may be harder to come up with these as you may never have thought about the person positively in these terms but give it your best shot now. Try for a maximum of five. Leave space for notes.

4 Against each of the person's strengths, give an example of when this has benefited you.

You may have found it harder to think of strengths than shortfalls. We often find it easier to identify negative aspects of a job or someone's performance – even our own. Just ask someone 'How's work?' and you'll see what I mean!

There are always strengths there as well – always. Think how you feel when you succeed at something – when you really consider that you've achieved your goal, even on occasion surpassed it. That whoopee feeling again! Your boss/partner/best friend feels that way too. When was the last time you said 'well done' to somebody? Try it more often – it works wonders.

Do you find it strange thinking about somebody's strength or skills in terms of the benefits it brings to others? If we're thinking assertively – perhaps it is strange. If we're thinking co-operatively – that's the holistic benefit which is gained by bringing individual talents together.

Belonging/assertion/co-operation

Future planning and realization follows a basic three-step path.

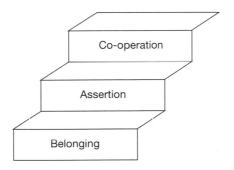

Let's consider it in sheep terms, for a start.

Belonging

When you start in a new job, you expect to have a work location – a desk, locker or operational area – which you can think of as your own personal space. It gives you confidence when you come in every morning, knowing you can go straight to that particular place. You feel you *belong*.

You've had your introduction to the company and been given some work to do. You may well have been teamed up with a 'buddy' colleague – or your supervisor or manager may even take on the role – to answer your immediate questions and help you be an active member of the workforce as quickly and painlessly as possible.

That's the *belonging* stage.

After a while of belonging, you begin to settle in – feel confident that you can take a more active part.

- You may feel ready to try some new activities – take on a bit more responsibility, perhaps.

- You might feel that you have some skill which you are not getting the chance to practise.

■ You might think you have spotted a slightly different way of achieving some business outcome and want to air your brilliant ideas.

This is where you begin to move towards the stage of *assertion*.

Assertion

Assertion doesn't have to be 'in yer face' to be successful. As a transition from *belonging* and a staging post towards *co-operation*, it's a way of putting forward these good ideas; of offering additional skills; of asking for some additional responsibility. It's bringing new opportunities and outcomes to the team or departmental pot.

Team leaders and bosses usually like staff members who think positively and who volunteer for extra involvement. You can assert these quite confidently at team meetings or by keeping your ear to the ground regarding present and future activities within the department.

Sheep-style *assertion* should thus be seen more in terms of adding your skills to the communal pot – not elbowing others aside to reach the front of the queue.

■ Be aware of the office politics though – don't try things in spite of (or worse still, to spite) others.

■ There are sometimes good reasons why things are done in a certain way – check them out first.

■ Remember that you want that first raising of your poppy head above the field to be successful, otherwise … swish!

■ Quietly find out a bit of the background before surging forward.

■ Tailor your first attempt to both fit in with – and improve – the current system.

Real change takes time to get going – but once it's moving, just try and stop it.

Assertion – or assertiveness as it is often called – has something of a bad reputation in certain quarters, thanks to some of the products of assertiveness training courses! These courses were originally designed to encourage people who had become stuck in the 'belonging' furrow, to gain the confidence to push themselves forward more.

Unfortunately, it also attracted some who were already naturally assertive but who wanted to become even more so – on the assumption that high octane assertion (verging on naked aggression) is the end game. Don't believe that. Being obstructive all the time might allow you to get your own way – it might seem amusing in some of the office sit.coms when it's happening to other people – but it's not the way forward in our brilliant future life.

You might have heard of the different ways of negotiating – *win/lose, lose/win* and so on. If you've studied it at all, you'll know that current thinking favours a *win/win* outcome, where both parties feel that they've succeeded to some degree. Obviously, there needs to be some give and take in order to arrive at an acceptable compromise – but the solution's more likely to stick.

History is littered with examples of enforced settlements which suffer ongoing relapses. Learn from these, apply *win/win* attitudes in your day-to-day life and try to take all aspects into consideration before reaching decisions – it makes it easier for people to work and live together – and encourages mutual support in the long term.

Work out time-5

In *Win/Win* thinking, the different parties are trying to reach a compromise agreement that's acceptable to the majority – or ideally, all. You can plan strategies for this, without the need to stick to them blindly during the event. It does help in the heat of the discussion if you have a variety of options at your fingertips and have thought through some of the implications. Time to make notes again!

1 Think of a fairly straightforward (sheep) situation where you want something to happen.

(For example, it might be that you want to leave work early or that you would like to attend a particular personal development event.) It is probably easier if you think of something within a business company framework. If you're currently a goat you may well have past sheep-type experience to call upon here.

Write down the key detail of your chosen situation.

_____

_____

_____

_____

2 Once you're clear in your mind what the situation is – and what the pre-ferred outcome will be for you – you're ready to make notes in two columns:

■ *Column One* sets out the things that are really important to you regarding the outcome

■ *Column Two* states the things which you are more likely to concede, as well as describing actions, etc which you can potentially use to trade.

Column One	Column Two

3 Finally, look at the key issues you have identified in Column One and stick a priority number against each one, with '1' as the one you're most likely to fight to the death over!

4 Now you've got your ammunition ready for your discussion, are clear on your priorities and have a few possible strategies up your sleeve. You will be more successful.

So, using the *Win/Win* strategy will help you assert yourself towards better, more workable solutions, without making enemies in the process.

Returning to our sheep scenario, you're now at the stage of applying assertion in order to 'sell your wares'; get yourself involved in more interesting activities with as much responsibility as you want – and identify areas and skills that you may wish to develop further.

At this point, it's important to consider the overall picture again, where the whole (or overall outcome) is worth more than the sum of the parts. That might sound a bit trite, like a mathematical equation – but the implications are very great.

In our sheep context, if various members of the department are providing different skills, this obviously broadens the scope – and raises the overall quality – of the department's performance. Also, some of these skills will intertwine, with individuals helping each other to progress further. How often have you seen people helping each other conquer some computer problem – not through formalized training but just by giving some assistance in passing to help their colleague over the next hurdle?

That's *co-operation* in action.

Co-operation

Chill out time-5

Think of a time when you were part of a group, working towards a common goal. It could be a team project you worked on, a team game, an oil drum raft exercise, or participating in some meeting to gain a contract for the company or your department.

Think how people worked together and the different skills they provided.

Focus on the assets and benefits that you and other individuals brought to the activity.

Focus on how these interlinked to form a better outcome.

Picture the positive responses which you received from the clients, judges or other participants. That's the *whoopee* factor we gain from co-operating with others.

Once started, co-operation is something which can just keep on going, as long as we can maintain the positive attitudes of those involved – and make sure that others don't take advantage of them. It needs support from senior managers – for example, people involved in coaching or mentoring others will need a bit of flexibility with their own workloads. It's more a state of mind than a technical science, and you have to work at changing the attitudes of some people.

Belonging/assertion/co-operation for goats

The belonging/assertion/co-operation thing works the same in goat-type thinking as well – although some of the people involvement happens in different ways.

When you start off being self-employed, your initial focus is very much on setting up the business. You gain excitement from having your own office or workplace, buying the necessary equipment and setting up the initial advertising and marketing. In a sense, instead of the (sheep) feeling where you are belonging to the company and fitting into its ways, in self employment you are able to create the environment which suits you. You feel that the company belongs to you rather than the other way round. The end result is still one of identifying closely with the business.

The next stage requires you to assert yourself through selling, networking and other means of bringing in the business. Selling is a special form of assertion, which can be quite complicated nowadays. If you're self-employed, you may either be on your own or have a small number of employees. The type of involvement with the group will vary depending on the situation. If you've been involved in Customer Care training, you may have considered the concept of customers being 'internal' as well as 'external'.

In sheep terms, internal customers are the colleagues that you have been working alongside, sharing skills and knowledge. If, as a self-employed goat, you have any internal customers, it is possible that these are sub-contracted services which you buy in as required. In this situation you're paying them, so are in a stronger position to assert your needs. You want a long-term working relationship with them, so it doesn't do to be too assertive. Self-employed professionals have an added motivation to compromise positively with each other and their customers.

You have to assert yourself with the external customer – the client – as well. But this will certainly be a softer form of assertion, through giving effective sales presentations, showing how professional you are during your initial discussions, or handling your win/win negotiations in the way we've already discussed.

Varying degrees of assertion can be applied in selling techniques. As with sheep thinking, the goat form of assertion is through showing confidently that you know your subject and that you can produce the goods. The co-operation level comes where you also show that you can adapt flexibly to meet the particular needs of the client – and encourage flexibility on their part also. Because you are in control of making the rules, you can flex your work, business or even pricing structures to suit the client's needs. That's the kind of co-operation that the client welcomes – and which can give you the selling edge over some of the bigger but more procedure-driven sheep.

So, we still have the three stages present – it just means that your strengths appear in a slightly different way.

Evaluating your own strengths and shortfalls

We've already considered the strengths and shortfalls of someone you know, working on the basis that it is always easier to judge someone other than yourself! It's now time to look at yourself in the mirror again. Don't get too bogged down in the detail of this exercise – remember it's your immediate reactions which count. You'll get a chance to review and analyse them later. You'll be answering this as either a sheep or a goat – each with slightly different bias.

Remember too that, when you are identifying your strengths, some could lie outside your direct work. You may, for example, be a wonderful chairperson for the local community council – and transfer these skills to leading your team meetings at work.

Note down your responses.

Find out time-6

1 What is your key strength?

_____

2 How do you apply this best in a working environment?

_____

3 List at least another three main strengths that you have.

_____

4 Which ones relate to dealing with people generally?

_____

5 Which one of these is your most valuable asset?

_____

6 What's your greatest strength when dealing with external customers?

_____

7 List your five main shortfall areas.

_____

8 Identify any of these which prevent you from working effectively.

9 Against each of these identified, note how you can improve the situation.

10 Where any shortfall area is hard to improve effectively, are there ways you can avoid using it? Note these.

We'll consider the shortfall areas more deeply slightly later. First, however, let's focus on your strengths.

You've had a stab at analysing your key strengths and identifying the ones that are most valuable in working along with others.

Find out time-7

Select one strength, focus on it and try to establish any elements you could develop further.

(You might feel, for example, that you are good at discussing problems with people and analysing potential solutions but are shy at making the initial approaches.)

Taking one of your own strengths, identify the area you would like to develop further and note down all the possible methods which come to mind.

***

The point here is that you're not settling back, living off your past successes. Instead, you're keeping a close watch on your strengths – and sharpening them up where you think it's necessary. We'll see this in greater detail later when we consider CPD (Continuous Professional Development). This is fast becoming an integral part of sheep thinking and links in closely with individuals planning their future.

Work out time-6

Let's think through an example of someone sharpening and developing existing skills.

Bob has been working as a supervisor for some time now.

He is good at talking to and motivating the people that report to him as individuals and he always has a sympathetic ear if they have a problem.

He's nervous about speaking to people as a group – and the team meetings suffer as a result.

He's been given the chance to go on an Effective Presentations course – to learn how to design presentations, produce visuals, handle questions from the floor and so on.

Is this the best course for Bob's needs?

What would you say were his key requirements?

Through planning our brilliant future, we will also be much clearer about the direction we want to take – and the goals we want to achieve to improve the way we live.

Focus on the strengths which you have and the actions you want to make to improve or broaden each strength. Don't be misled into thinking that you need to continually expand your CPD range of skills. There is a difference between sensible personal development and change just for the sake of it. In our example above, Bob is not really involved in giving grand presentations. His greatest need is to learn how to chair or facilitate a meeting, how to make statements in a clear and precise way and how to handle people in the group in a way that encourages them to participate.

Ongoing personal and professional development should be broadening and refreshing your present skills. Keep up to date with the way things are moving in that current area of work – earn your living with that and you can afford to rely on others to provide the skills which don't interest you. Design a website? No problem. Dripping tap? Call a plumber.

We'll come back to the joys of working on your CPD later, when we look at the ways different companies and professions react. It's fair to say that it's early days yet and some of the judgements and criteria used are rather basic. All the more reason for you to know how to plan and manage your own brilliant future.

So, enough on your strengths for the moment – let's focus on the shortfalls.

Find out time-8

1   Write down between three and six headings which represent the various areas of involvement which you consider important in your life.

(They may be things like coping with – people, technology, family matters, health and physical wellbeing and so on. I'm sure there are others which are relevant to you.)

Priority 1:

_____

_____

_____

_____

_____

Priority 2:

_____

_____

_____

_____

_____

Priority 3:

_____

_____

_____

_____

_____

2   Under each heading, list areas (as specifically as possible) where you con-sider that you have a shortfall. (These could include things where an improvement would give you a personal buzz – such as your golf handicap or elements of your work which are, in all truth, below par – such as your competency at computer, lathe or whatever. It could be your people skills.) Think hard on this and include as many as possible.

3 It will be more realistic to develop some of these than others, for a variety of reasons. Looking through your shortfall lists, mark a 'Y' against the ones that you feel you can improve in any way at all in the near future. Mark an 'N' against those where you feel it will be very hard to achieve any marked improvement, regardless of time spent.

Work out time-7

1 Focus on these 'N' responses in 3 above. Identify any of them which, if you don't improve your performance, could get in the way of your brilliant future. These are your 'NHP' items – 'No – High Priority'.

(Be objective. You may need a bit of help here to maintain this objectivity – you're trying to isolate the shortfall areas which are a potential problem and which you'll have to do something about.)

2 You can set aside the other 'Ns' – as long as there aren't too many. Having too many 'don't dos' might make you rather vulnerable!

(If you're working co-operatively as a sheep, there's probably someone else that can do this particular skill, so the solution can come through delegation or worksharing. If you're a self-employed goat, you can always buy in a particular skill which is a personal 'N', if you really need it.)

Write down your 'NHPs' in the left-hand space below.

4 Where do I want to go?

It's time to think 'bigger picture'. You have your status quo, you do your work every day, you have activities which occupy your evenings and weekends, you've got some level of standard of living which you find acceptable (or not), you have some degree of job and life satisfaction.

In the visual terms we have been describing, you are at some point along the track, standing at the head of your meandering trail. A bit like a snail (in the nicest possible way!), with that trail glistening to show the past route you have taken. The parameters of the track – the hedges or fences – show the boundaries of your operational rules and regulations. Some of these will be general life standards, while others will relate to your present work involvement.

Find out time-9

1 Write down three key 'life standards' (of the 'Ten commandments' variety) which you live by and will continue to live by, regardless of the work you do or the life you will lead in the future. If you feel there are more than three, write as many as you feel strongly about.

2 Write down three 'work standards' which *you* have, that relate to the work you are currently doing.

---

3 Write down several different 'work standards' which might apply if you changed the direction of your path dramatically.

You might find the latter part a bit harder – and of course it is dependent on you having the idea that you want a change – and if so, what that change might be. But that's what this book is all about, after all.

Let's stick with this path idea for a while.

- Has your current variable journey along your path been an effort; have you had problems figuring out where you want to go?
- Have the detours been to get round blocks so that you can get back onto your decided path?
- If you have a decided path, is this heading as directly as it can towards the future you have established for yourself? If not – any strategies?

Focus and motivation

Where you are clearer on your future path, your focus and motivation are different, evidently, though neither one is right or wrong – or better or worse. Let's think through the two levels of goal focus for a moment, to see the difference.

Work out time-8

Let's say we have two men in their early twenties – both following time-honoured conventions and wanting to be an astronaut. For ease of reference, we'll call them Andy and Bob. Let's say that Andy really, really wants this – he has watched every available film and TV programme on space flight and travel and wrote to NASA some time ago to receive details of how to get on training programmes and so on.

Bob, on the other hand, progressively becomes more fascinated by the communications technology involved, when he thinks about it some more. Rather than specifically craving to be an astronaut, he finds himself attracted towards the Mission Control set-up and the range and variety of communications technologies which are being developed.

How clear would Andy's career path be?

What might some of the steps and stages of this path be?

What might the key challenges/blocks be?

How clear would Bob's career path be?

What might some of the steps and stages of this path be?

What might his key challenges/blocks be?

There are probably fairly set paths that Andy can follow – join the Air Force and train to become a fighter pilot or particular expert required on space programmes. Bob's path is going to meander a bit more, probably, with his general interest in space communications gradually focusing on some particular computer or telecoms area of activity which really hits his whoopee button.

Andy's work track boundaries will be pre-set, being those linked with both joining up and then progressing through the specialist training necessary to become an astronaut – he is clear on his final goal or objective. Bob's, on the other hand, will probably vary a bit. He may, for example, start off working for a government agency, then move over into the private sector, with more commercial opportunities. He might attempt to specialize in satellite technology but then realize that he is more interested in the digital telecoms area.

There's no right or wrong answer to this exercise – it's just a case of thinking through some of the differences, priorities and implications. It underscores the fact that, for some people, job selection and refinement in the earlier years of employment are part of the focusing process. Sometimes, you need to take a few faltering steps in a range of directions to sort out in your own mind what your preferred path really is. Of course, if you could figure it all out perfectly in theory, it would save time and effort, but few of us can, so trial and error rules OK sometimes.

What is your focus?

Now's the time to consider yourself very closely.

- You may be happy doing what you're currently doing.
- You may see a career path stretching out before you, which will happen naturally and within an acceptable time frame.
- You may be perfectly content with the status quo.

If that's the case – fine. If you do feel ready for a bit of change – equally, fine.

It certainly bears thinking about carefully – and let's face it, if you're reading this book, you must have some dynamic thoughts about developing a brilliant future, which may extend beyond your present scenario.

Chill out time-7

Give yourself a quiet 10 minutes somewhere.

Think about the life you're leading currently.

Can you see the direction you're taking?

Do you feel in control?

Is there anything you would like to change?

You've already thought through some of your own priorities, possible changes in direction and ways forward in some of the earlier exercises. You may want to check back at some of the responses you've already made or you may want to approach the situation from a slightly different and fresh direction. Make notes of your responses as you progress. It's up to you. This is empowerment.

Find out time-10

1   If you ever lie in bed thinking dynamic work activity thoughts, what are they about?

2   Do your plans indicate an interest that you'd like to spend more time doing?

3   If so, is there any way you could spend more of your working time applying them?

4   Is there any slight change of focus, within your present work scenario, which would help?

5 What actions could you take to get these plans moving?

---

6 Is there any personal development which would make the move easier?

---

7 If the change would involve a different type of job, how could you manage this change?

---

8 Are you really aware of the pros and cons of the activity and work you are targeting?

---

9 Are there specific milestones which chart the path between Now and this new work focus?

---

10 Is there anyone you can speak to who can fill in some of the missing detail and actions?

This is your future you're thinking about here, so take your time and think carefully.

Milestones

It's the stages along the path – the milestones – which are hard to identify sometimes. You may be quite clear on the end goal. Unfortunately, you will doubtless be aware of someone who has succeeded in a similar activity, apparently effortlessly. I'm sure that person would be the first to tell you that most of their 'good luck' has come from astute business thinking, having the finance available and knowing exactly how to get where they want to be – their end goal. Be aware that brilliant future planning is rewarded with what others think is brilliant luck.

It's establishing these milestones that's important. As we've already agreed, they remain flexible but you need to know how you're going to check whether you're getting there. And if you aren't, you need to be able to figure out how you can get moving in the right direction again.

Find out as much as you can about how people have achieved what you want to become. And don't dwell on the good luck stories. There are always those that got into television, or whatever, because their dad was already something in the industry – or managed to set up in business because of a gift of a large bag of money from some relation.

These are not the success stories you should interest yourself in pay attention to the ones where someone has figured out their own path and progressively gone for it, stage by stage. Take the television example – Media Studies graduates are two a penny now. It's no longer just having the degree that counts, it's the additional experience, projects and involvement which an individual has done which makes him or her stand out from the herd. Don't wait for good luck – plan, progress and manoeuvre.

These planned stages can take a long time to pass. The time element is one of the hardest and most confusing things in personal planning. Frustration can weaken motivation and distract the vision. Writing down your plans and referring to them regularly – with revision where necessary – will help you maintain your motivated vision. That's the power of planning. Done well, you:

- clarify your priorities
- set down your overall objective and goals
- plan your milestones
- identify methods of progressing
- pinpoint people that can help you along the way
- create ways of monitoring progress.

Breaking out

So far we've been concentrating more on changes in direction – implying that you may want to be detouring slightly within your present job, or looking for a sideways move with your present employer to allow you to do more of what takes your fancy, without changing employer or job in any major way. That's sheep thinking.

If you've got that bit of goat in you, you might be wanting to break through the hedge in a slightly more dynamic way. Change job completely, or move from employed to freelance. It's your decision – you have to think it through. If the previous FIND OUT exercise showed up some overwhelming area of interest which you'd like to turn your hand to, perhaps now's the time to figure out which direction is potentially best.

Work out time-9

Here are a few trigger thoughts to apply to three distinct sheep areas:

- moving within your present company
- moving to a new company
- setting up as freelance.

Moving within your present company

- Is there anything you can do (formally or informally) within your present job, to give you some experience in the work you want to do?
- As it is often easier to move jobs internally, how can you best make positive

contacts with the movers and shakers of the department you are targeting?

- Is there anything further you can find out about the internal job advertisement system used by your company – and how to use it to best advantage?
- Is there an internal communication system (company newsletter, etc) which you can use to sell yourself and your successes more?

Moving to a new company

- If you have a particular company/companies in mind, is there any way you can register your interest and CV detail and keep that information in their active file?
- Are you aware of the range of agencies and newspaper/online advertisements which you must monitor and respond to regularly?
- Have you updated your CV in line with the type of job you are trying to get (as opposed to the job you are currently in, which might have different priorities)?
- Is there anything you can do in the meantime to make yourself more job-attractive – development training, studying for professional qualification, etc?

Setting up as freelance

- Would you have access to the technology and facilities necessary to do your chosen work freelance?
- Are you aware of a range of potential clients which you can expect work from in the first few months of setting up?
- Can you work out a business plan that convinces *you* that you will manage to clear enough income to live off?
- What is it that you can provide which is better than your direct competition?

Moving into freelance working is goat thinking, if ever there was – but of course it extends even further than that, if you've already set up as freelance or self-employed and are thinking of expansion or a change in emphasis.

There are considerations such as:

- is your new concept sustainable – might you be supporting a loss-making new idea for an extended period – which could cripple your core business?
- is it using existing facilities and resources (making them more cost effective) or is it requiring new capital expenditure, which could bomb if the concept fails?
- would you need to take on more staff?
- how does this new concept tie in with your existing business – can you use the one to give added value to the other?

Some of these might sound a bit weighty – but they are important to consider when you are deciding on a new direction. It's the sort of stuff you would be asked if you went to a business adviser – or your friendly bank manager, if you were looking for a business start-up loan. Thinking about it now will save you sitting like a twit in the bank manager's office, realizing you haven't really got the answers.

Are you ready for a change?

So, having looked at the possibilities from different angles and considered as gently as possible whether you feel the need for a change, we're reaching crunch time. What's it going to be? Is change an option? Is your family/domestic/financial situation ready to cope with this level of change? Do you really feel up for it? If you do, which direction do you feel happiest trying?

Chill out time-8

This is a CHILL OUT rather than a FIND OUT because you really need some peaceful, objective thinking here – not racing against time or feeling under pressure, just puzzling your way through the options and thinking with your heart rather than your head for a while. Try it – it works!

Just a few thoughts to kick around for a while.

- What do I really want to do with my life?
- Can my family/domestic life cope with it?
- What do I need to do to prepare the way?
- How do I best pursue what I really want to do?
- When's the best time to make the change?
- What's the first thing I have to do next?

So, you've now considered your present situation, your hopes and aspirations, your strengths and a few of the possible blocks (including your own shortfalls) from a variety of different angles.

You should be pretty clear, in your heart of hearts, where you want to go in your own future. If not, Chill Out for a little longer. There are still unanswered questions.

Don't feel you *have to* set off into the great unknown. Even if you're planning your progress within your present situation, you can still find ways to spice up your *whoopee* factor.

How can you:

- build confidence so that you enjoy doing what you are doing?
- plan milestones so that you can see some progress ahead?
- set goals so that you get a buzz achieving them?

If you do feel you want to change direction, though, there are extra possibilities out there, waiting to be found. Go and look for them.

So that we can really focus, let's take the stance that you feel that you can change fairly dramatically, for this next exercise. Let's do it. Make notes as you progress.

Find out time-11

1   What's your best skill?

_____

2   What real proof have you got that you can do it well?

_____

3   How would you like to use this to better advantage?

_____

4   What other skills do you have which would help achieve this?

_____

5   What preparations will you need to achieve, so that it can begin to happen?

_____

6   What extra experience do you need, which will help you get where you want to go?

_____

7   How do you go about gaining this?

_____

8   Are there intermediate stages you should achieve between Now and your ideal?

_____

9 What strategy can you develop to travel this route?

10 If you really want this to happen, what are your first three milestones for the next three months?

Take your time to think through these answers.

Teamwork

So far, we've been thinking about you:

- you as an individual
- what you can do to progress yourself
- how you can go where you want to go.

However, life's a bit more complex than this. We don't live and work in a bubble. There are others around. They're reading their copy of this book too so they're all individuals sorting out their paths along the track. They're also at different stages in the belonging/assertion/co-operation process, just to make things more complicated.

So, at this stage in development, we need to start thinking a little about living and working with others – and how we can do it more effectively as well. There are lots of books and courses around which examine team building in much greater detail than I intend to do – sort people into categories – give them labels and go through a host of exercises to prove that a mix of skills gives the best type of team.

We're working on the basis here that any individual – you, for example – is a fairly complex being.

- Most individuals are capable of both planning and doing activities.
- Most individuals can be proactive to some extent, if given the opportunities.

■ Many theoreticians will know how to carry out the practical proof – even though they would prefer others to do the manipulation and construction – and could make a go of it, if pressed.

■ Some activists would consider that finding a solution by trial and error rather than detailed planning has benefits – and find support from some educational theory quarters. Trial and error still involves planning.

In short, each of us is potentially a mix of different skills, knowledge and experience which we can achieve to different degrees. Combining these mixtures still further within a group or team will give us an even more potent and effective blend – reaching explosive levels, ultimately! That's the effect of objective co-operation.

We've already mentioned this effect, where the end result is worth more than the sum of the parts. It applies when you take the different competencies of an individual and mould them together. It applies more obviously when you bring a bunch of people together in a team, with strengths and shortfalls levelling out overall.

Work out time-10

Let's say I'm good at analysing things and setting the findings down in reports – but I'm not so good at knocking on doors, encouraging people to participate.

Let's say you're good at presenting findings and leading discussions round to agreements – but get bored working through all the detail and setting it out in reports.

Let's say that Margaret across there has got a very logical mind and has been involved in the processes we are using over a period of time – but hates speaking in public.

Let's say that Simon in the corner has worked out in the field and has seen the processes applied effectively … and less than effectively in different processes. He's not too keen on spending lots of time in committee meetings though.

If you were setting up a project team to look into current process applications, rationalise these to become the 'company standard processes' and then make sure that these are applied uniformly throughout the company –

- how would you use these people in your team?
- what other team members/skills might you require?
- how would you go about achieving the goal above?

You've worked in teams or with others. Maybe not in a formal project team or whatever – but certainly having to take note of what others say and want. However good a team player you are, however strongly we think 'holistic co-operation', there are times when working with others is a real pain in the neck.

Find out time-12

1 Have you had a bad experience working with others in a group?

2 What was the problem?

3 What do you think the cause was – participants/environment/resources/ timescale, etc?

4 What was the immediate effect?

5 How was the problem finally resolved – and how did this link with the causes in 3 above?

---

6 What lessons did you learn?

---

7 How could the group have been organized better?

---

8 Would a more balanced mix of skills etc have helped? If so, how?

---

9 Would you have changed the group composition and dynamics in any ways?

---

10 How could you have performed differently, to give an improved end result overall?

It's fair to say that each one of us could probably perform better within a group than we do currently, if we tried – better for the group outcome, that is. It's not all compromise. If we think back to the ideas of team working, the idea is that we're progressing through assertion to co-operation. Is progress a one-way street?

Not necessarily. Think of assertion as the positive act of getting across your capabilities, priorities and desires. You can do this within a group so that you can play a more active part. Sometimes, no-one wants to push themselves forward and take the lead in a democratic group. Groups need leaders and volunteers to get moving. So, there are times where a bit of gentle assertion can help get a co-operatively-working group moving forward. Then you can revert to co-operative progress again.

It's likely that the future plans you're working on will involve others – unless a cave on an Outer Hebrides island beckons. So, some of your planning should focus on how you can work and exist with people at the moment – and how this might extend as time passes. How important this is will depend a bit on what you're planning to do. It certainly needs some thought.

Work out time-11

1   How do your future plans involve working with others?

2   Do you foresee any problems?

3   What skills and shortfalls might you have to develop, to work better in the group?

4   What strengths do you have as a team player?

5   What strengths in others would you hope to link with, for a better holistic group effect?

6   What benefits will you gain from working with others?

---

7   What benefits can you bring to the group?

---

8   What's the first step?

So, there are decisions to be made as an individual as well as decisions as a team player.

Summary

You've moved on down your path during this chapter – and the previous ones. You should be a lot clearer about:

- direction
- priorities
- development needs
- involvement with others
- working co-operatively.

If you're not, read through the chapter again and have another go at some of the exercises. It's worth sorting this stage out before moving on to the next, which is to be able to establish your milestones and goals as clearly as possible. Next chapter, we're thinking objectives.

Chill out time-9

Take a break.

Think of some of the milestones you've already passed – and some of your future ones.

part two

view
your
options

Here, we want to think closely about how you can progress most effectively – what techniques and methods suit you best; how you can make the most of the facilities on offer. Finally, we'll review the best ways of organizing and recording all this detail.

5 Under the microscope

Getting the message across is very important. Communication is key. Being as clear and precise as possible cuts down on confusion. Cutting out the spin and focusing on truth generates trust. Being clear on your goals or milestones speeds progress.

A delegate on one of my seminars came out with the memorable phrase:

'If you aim at nothing, you're sure to hit it'.

It's true, of course – and a means of justifying any action … in hindsight. But that's not what we're about. We want to be clear about where we're heading, so that we can check on progress, communicate equally with others … and make adjustments to keep that progress moving.

Objectives

You have probably come across at least some of the following types of objectives:

- business objectives
- departmental objectives
- learning objectives
- programme objectives
- personal objectives
- production objectives
- appraisal objectives.

They're also called different jargon-ny titles in business sometimes – not always meaning exactly the same – but covering the same ideas. There are:

- goals
- targets
- competencies
- CPD outcomes (Continuing Professional Development)

and doubtless other new titles which are being dreamed up at this very moment. All attempts to get specific statements so that everyone involved is singing from the same hymn sheet, so to speak.

We're going to look at objectives in some detail because they are the foundation on which our plans are built.

Work out time-12

So – what exactly is an objective?

It's a precise statement which describes an outcome or end point. If I'm your manager, mentor, coach, trainer or whatever, we can use it together to set your individual goal or target – a point 'X' – for you to achieve. If the wording is precise, there will be no doubts about when you have reached that point 'X', so we'll both be happy. We'll both be able to check how you're progressing towards this point 'X' as well by having an idea of the milestones along the way. And we'll be able to match how well you've achieved your objectives against the expected stages of progress – both of others and the business generally.

At an individual level, you can personally think in an objective way, giving yourself the goals, milestones and other checks and balances to monitor how you're getting on. Useful stuff, eh?

How do we write a suitable precise statement?

We're looking to include:

- an end point, outcome or output (a result or product)
- action(s) involved in getting there
- a standard which can and will be achieved – and which can be measured
- any ground rules or restrictions for carrying out the actions.

The simplest kinds of learning objectives are ones which set down a task to be done.

Traditionally, trainers speak about 'widgets', meaning anything you're producing as part of your work activities. So, if I wanted to train you to operate a 'widget making machine' to produce enough widgets to the acceptable standard, the objective might be something like:

'Operating the widget making machine as set down in the manual, produce 25 widgets per hour to meet the international widget standard (IWS), with a maximum of 10% waste'.

So you have:
- *end point/output:* widgets
- *action:* produce widgets by operating the machine
- *standard:* operation as manual; produce 25 per hour; meet IWS; have a maximum of 10% waste
- *ground rules:* use of specified machine type, having raw materials available.

If I were to write a personal objective for you to identify, it might be along the lines of:
'List four of your key strengths, describing each in terms of how you can apply it in your work and how you can measure your performance against a stated level of achievement'.

- Identify the actions and other reference points in the statement.
    -
    -
    -

■ Write a personal objective to establish one of your shortfall areas.

   ■

   ■

   ■

Tying in your objectives

We've spoken about individuals and co-operative teams – where the individuals' efforts build to a combined team effort plus additional holistic (outcome is greater than the parts) benefits, which go towards achieving some business target which the company has set.

By substituting the word 'objective(s)' for 'effort(s)' and 'target' in the previous sentence: 'We've spoken about individuals and co-operative teams – where the individuals' objectives build to a combined team objective plus additional holistic benefits, which go towards achieving some business objective which the company has set.' you can see how individual, departmental and business objectives marry together. Statements will be different but – if they're precise – they'll mix and match, to achieve the overall objective (that 'O' word again!)

Work out time-13

Let's say you are one of a team producing widgets.

Your department produces the Mark Two Thing, which requires five widgets per Thing.

Your company manufactures Dodgy Devices, each of which uses two Things in its design. The company objective/target is to produce 200 complete Dodgy Devices per working day.

A bit of simple maths here: in order to meet the Company production objective –

■ How many Mark Two Things must your department produce daily?

- How many Widgets must you (i.e. the total widget line) produce daily?

These must meet the set-down standards – so the waste factor will have to be included, to guarantee there are enough usable components each production day.

So, each production day, we need a minimum of 400 Things and 2000 widgets to be produced, all meeting these international standards. If there are, say, five members in your widget production line, each person (including you) will have the individual objective of producing 400 acceptable widgets per day.

That's a very simple example of how the outcomes of individual, team, department and company/business objectives tie together. The 'widget' doesn't have to be a physical thing. It could be a change order to be processed; a sale to be closed; a financial or insurance transaction to be agreed. The objective principle remains the same.

In the example, if you don't manage to meet your objective of producing 400 usable widgets per day, the company will not be able to meet its production objective of 200 complete products per day, especially if it applies Just In Time production techniques.

Looking at it from the development point of view, it is crucially important to the company that your skills level allows you to produce this output level consistently. So, any training requests which focus on this skill are more likely to be supported by the company. On the other hand, if you personally felt the need to attend a Customer First course or study basic Excel, you might find it harder to justify your personal objectives against the business objectives of the company. So you might not get the support you hoped for. Personal and professional objectives work best when they marry together – largely because this allows the practical reinforcement to happen. The link also shows that sometimes, there are reasons why you have to do something in a certain way – to slot into the bigger picture.

The value of objectives

Objective thinking helps you reason and plan in a logical sequence, too. That's helpful when you're trying to learn something. Bloom's *Taxonomy of Objectives* sets out knowledge objectives in a sequence:

- knowing specifics
- understanding
- doing
- analysing
- applying in new situations
- making judgements.

That means, when you're planning your own development, you should try to think in this way – knowing the basics before getting the key detail; taking some time to figure out the theory before you get involved in the all-important practical reinforcement. In some cases, that's as far as we might progress.

If we're getting to a more advanced stage, we can then use our knowledge to figure out steps and stages and then move on to using this awareness to build new models. So, for example, we could use our knowledge of negotiating skills to see which steps in our discussions weren't working – and then build a new argument. After more experience, we could reach the stage of judging negotiations confidently.

Thinking in an objective way helps you:

- think logically
- see how things link together
- plan so that learning builds in a progression
- specify what it is you want to do
- establish indicators to look out for
- set goals and targets
- identify blocks and do something about them.

It encourages you to think in actions, as well. Look at the first word of each of these bullet points above. It gets you thinking about what to *do*, doesn't it? Thinking, writing and speaking in action verbs helps us move forward more positively, more precisely.

For example, if I were to say that I'll talk to you for the next 10 minutes to 'help you appreciate some of the important elements of writing objectives', that doesn't give us much of a milestone to head for, docs it? What does 'appreciate' mean? What exactly are the elements? Important for what? It's all a bit vague.

Putting objective thinking into practice

So, now it's time to think specific objectives for your brilliant future. Soon, we'll be taking the first steps of transferring some of your notes into the more structured ID Plan. We're aiming to write these entries clearly and precisely, as well as having them cross-relate with each other – which is why we're focusing on objectives at the moment.

Find out time-13

1   Think of your strengths and shortfalls again – you considered these in *FIND OUT Time 6*, on page 40. Review the list you made.

2   Select two of your strengths and write an action which you will take to develop these still further.

3   Do the same for two of your shortfall areas.

4 Identify something which you have on your 'Things to Do' list … (you must have one, even if it's just a scrap of paper on your desk or a note in your diary … or the back of your hand). Write down what you hope to achieve – as precisely as possible.

Your note might say 'Call Geoff'. But what for? What's the outcome or result you want? Is there any flexibility? If so, what things are you less bothered about?

I'm not suggesting you set down detail like this for each of the things on your 'things to do' list – otherwise it would become a 'things to do' notebook in its own right, or you'd have to start writing up your arm, rather than just on the back of your hand. What I am suggesting is, if you have thought of some of the targets and milestones before you pick up the 'phone, you'll be a lot more positive and focused. You'll also be ready for some of the counter arguments, so you don't get in the situation of thinking, three minutes after putting the phone down, 'If I'd said so-and-so then, when he said that … I would have got what I wanted.' Too late. That's the application of positive assertion again – being able to move things forward confidently in the direction you want. But still reaching a co-operative result.

Let's focus on the three initial levels of objectives for a moment:

- knowledge
- understanding
- application.

This is for areas of development where you're building knowledge. (If you want to impress people at parties, they're called 'Cognitive Objectives'.)

Understanding and applying these three steps in the correct sequence will help you be successful in your own development. It will

also help if you become involved as a coach or mentor, helping someone else with their development.

Work out time-14

A simple operational example first. Remember our 'Widget Making Machine',
which we were required to operate 'as set down in the manual'? If you were
teaching someone how to do that (rather than just tossing the manual towards
him), how would you go about it?

You might go through the following steps:

- identify the controls
- indicate the steps and stages of the widget making process
- state the health and safety considerations.

These are all initial knowledge levels. Know where the on and off buttons are;
any adjustments which are needed to keep the product within the international standards; be aware of the steps and stages of the process and how
these tie in with the actual machine. And then, of course, know when to keep
fingers out of the machine; not to breathe in the dust ... and the other safety
precautions which must be stated, to prove that the machine owner has met
the requirements.

Once the factual foundations are laid, you can move on to the understanding levels:

- know what the controls do
- apply the benefits of fine-tuning the controls
- follow through the steps and stages of the operation
- identify standards of operation and production.

So far, we can do all this without switching on the machine. Take the four 'understanding' examples. Now, imagine that we've switched on the machine and can
(slowly) produce one or two items of the product, to test out the process.
Because we are doing it and can see something happening, as learners, our
understanding can improve. Think of the action verbs:

- *operate* the controls
- *fine-tune* the controls to maintain production
- *follow* through the steps and stages of the operation
- *monitor* standards of operation and production.

There's progress. There's even more subdivision when you're mentoring or coaching somebody in the process. If someone is learning how to operate something, the normal stages in development are:

- trainer demonstrates the steps singly and separately
- trainer demonstrates the steps slowly, as a sequence
- learner goes through the steps, with guidance
- learner practises – supervised as necessary.

Have you ever asked a computer whiz-kid how to do something, only to be met with a flurry of their fingers on the keyboard, coupled with the 'instruction' – 'You just do it like this – whirrrrrrrrrrrrrrr – it's simple really. OK? You'll manage OK – Bye'?

Now you see why the steps – and actually getting a chance to try things out, with a bit of support – are very important. They give you a series of milestones – and make sure that you pause for a while at each one, to let the learning sink in. The same sequence works if you're learning something yourself – or developing a skill. You can speed up some of the practical stages, sometimes, because you can then focus on the areas you find hard. You'd be practising these bits until you're sure that you can do them, or understand them. The secret of success is still thinking actions – and small learning stages. Think of them as 'bite sized chunks' – there's a good mental picture to keep in front of you.

So, that's a quick romp through the structure of practical objectives. When you move from operating machines and such-like to learning new information, you're then moving into the knowledge (or Cognitive) areas. The structures are much the same, as are the priorities of actions, steps and stages and the pauses for reinforcement. There are one or two differences which a short example will demonstrate.

Work out time-15

Let's say you want to learn how to write a technical type of report, following a set structure and including a range of information and results (or outcomes).

If you flick backwards and forwards between this and the previous widget example (*WORK OUT Time 14*) you should be able to follow the similarities.

At the first, *knowledge* level, you'd be thinking about the structure of the report:

■ the different headings that are required
■ the preferred layout
■ whether conclusions or recommendations are included
■ the types of information included in any appendix.

That's facts and information – so that you know the language and names which are used – and basically what each means.

Then you move on to *understanding*. You would have to go into greater depth here, learning what the different headings actually mean: Terms of Reference; Recommendations; Methods of Investigation. You'd have to understand *why* certain layouts are used and when something like an executive summary is needed. In short, you'll be getting a good understanding of how a report is put together and the reasons and uses for the different bits.

So, what do you think you would include in the *application* section of this learning?

What kind of practical reinforcement would be useful?

You're the imagined learner in this example. If you think about it, what examples and exercises could you do which would help you achieve your objective?

And what would that objective be?

It should be much along the lines of the statement in the first sentence of this exercise.

There's loads more we could do but that's probably enough for our needs at the moment. The examples are from the learning development stable, rather than business objectives, but the same basic principles apply.

Attitude objectives

Changing people's attitudes can be a lot harder than adding to their knowledge. Why? Because people are coming from all kinds of different angles and starting points and often need time to accept change – if they decide they want to change, that is. But it's very important to be aware of these different attitudes. It's also very important to try to do something about persuading any doubters about your grand new policy, before you start waxing eloquent about how good it is. Otherwise, some sets of ears will be switched off from the start – and there's no way you will convert and convince them.

Let's say that one of your development objectives will only work properly if other people do things in a different way as well. It might be that you decide that you will only respond to e-mails sent specifically to you, deleting all the chain letter types without reading them.

This will make your communication time more efficient. Your policy won't please everyone though, once you have made it known generally. You'll meet a range of attitudes. You'll have to justify your decision in different ways to different people – on occasion, you may have to bend your stance or even accept that some business policy updates, etc must be published in a circular copy form. You need that sort of information as you can't do your job if you don't have it. There's the importance of compromise and co-operation again. That's responding to attitudes specifically.

Many of the blocks you'll come across in your future planning will be caused by the attitudes of others. Take time to listen to and consider the particular attitude blocking your way. Assume nothing. Consider how it impacts with your stance and attitude – and find a way round it. Some people's attitudes and stances mirror the 'official' way of thinking, others will have a political agenda, which could give it a totally different angle from your own viewpoint. If you're a right brain thinker, it can be a problem working with these people – as they're hard to influence. And it's hard for you to travel your path in a deep wheel rut. Keep trying to move forward – and out. But travel gently. Once you've proved once or twice that your way has greater flexibility, or that you're open to acceptable compromise – and you can point to past examples where officialdom has come round to your way of thinking … Bingo!

Chill out time-10

Spend a moment thinking where you are at the moment, in your own development.

Focus on a particular area which you want to develop.

Think of one or two targets you can set yourself.

Figure out – objectively – how you can progress towards these targets.

Objectives and team working

We've seen that objective thinking:

- helps you stay focused
- encourages logical steps and stages
- gives you targets and milestones
- helps people with common aims work together
- aids your forward planning
- links different levels of a project together.

We've touched on teamwork and on how individual plans can link together for optimum overall effect. Objective thinking can help here as well. If we're thinking co-operatively – which we are – it's the overall end point that's important. It's the combination of skills and the times when individual paths can merge together. And, when these skills do merge, the group of individuals will experience a great surge forward. I've come across assertive thinkers who are disturbed by this idea.

'I must surge forward faster than the rest, or I'm not succeeding.'

Whoop ... whoop ... whoop. Flashing red light. Attitude change needed here.

As I said at the start of this book, it's not necessary to step on the heads of other climbers to reach the top of the mountain. We're thinking co-operative brilliant futures here. Sure, your progress can be helped by the efforts of others. But that's only part of the deal. Holistic thinking is looking for your input into the common pot as well – finishing up with a better result for all. Link your skills with the skills of others – don't suck their energy out for your own ends.

If you are up there co-operating with others, there may still be times when you have to regress to asserting your ideas more positively. This may become necessary, from time to time, to reach that acceptable compromise with other assertive voices. However, once the eddies have settled and the flow returns to normal, co-operative progress can come into play once more.

Know when self-promotion is needed – but also when acceptance is the best reply.

Work out time-16

Have you ever worked in a team which was a bit chaotic? Perhaps you have had experience of the following.

- Others overlapping with work you had thought was your responsibility.
- Work being repeated, and perhaps done in different ways.
- Periods of doing nothing, waiting for decisions to be made.
- The goalposts being shifted, with completed work scrapped.
- Some team members doing a lot more of the work than others.
- Team members having long chats while you are trying to work.
- People doing things which could be done much better by others.
- Deadlines being missed because there's no controls on the schedule.

Can you think of any more problems that you may have experienced?
From your knowledge of objective thinking now, make notes of how you could apply this to improve on some of these problems.

Some of the areas you should think about might include:

- individual responsibilities
- links between these responsibilities
- targets, objectives and milestones
- need for reviews and revisions
- some kind of project planning
- monitoring and controls to keep things moving forward.

Summary

Thinking in an objective way helps you as an individual to get your act together – and keeps you moving on down the development path. Individuals thinking objectively in a co-operative way will get the team working together well which will help them achieve some level of holistic result – where the end is worth more than the sum of the parts.

6   How do I advance?

Where have we got to so far?

You've been considering yourself pretty closely during these last few chapters, highlighting some of your best bits and more suspect bits; perhaps putting your finger on something which will give that old whoopee factor again and gathering some initial ideas together as to how you should be planning your future and setting it down.

You've got your foundations bedded down pretty solidly and you've begun to have a fairly clear view of how your chosen milestones stand up along your preferred path. You're capable of thinking – and writing – these views in a precise, objective way. You'll need as much practice as possible (which your life will make sure you get), to help your objective way of thinking sharpen up, but the potential's there. The actual direction you'll take – and the way you'll take it – will vary a bit depending on whether you're on your own, doing it personally or professionally, or perhaps doing it as an employee within a company.

Development through learning

It may be that one of the easiest ways of helping yourself to move from where you are to where you want to be is by developing your skills and knowledge (either to build on a strength or address a shortfall) through some form of learning. If your immediate reaction is: 'but I haven't got time to go on a course', the next exercise should prove that there are other alternatives.

Chill out time-11

Think about how you learn, generally.

What are some of the different ways you could learn? They might include:

- reading books
- talking to people
- watching programmes on TV
- doing Open University/Distance Learning style programmes
- going on short courses
- doing some form of college course
- attending training provided by your place of work
- getting a demonstration from somebody
- doing some form of practice at a practical skill
- figuring things out for yourself
- surfing the net.

The list could go on – you may have some other preferred ways.

Think about it for a while.

Which ways do you prefer to learn?

You may have thought of some informal learning methods such as:

- teaming up with a buddy so that he or she can help you along the way with a bit of advice here, or a demonstration there
- coaching – where somebody can help you develop your own skill by working along with you
- having a mentor, who brings his or her skill, knowledge and experience to the table and shows you how to work smarter
- learning through co-operating in a team.

We are going to look at *mentoring* and *coaching* in detail in Chapter 9, so for now we will concentrate on the other, more formal learning methods.

The learning technique you choose for any learning you want to do will depend on several factors, including:

- what it is you want to learn (learning objectives)
- what learning activities are available (learning facilities)
- your preference
- your budget and development support (learning resources).

What do you want to learn?

Objective thinking is a useful technique for pinpointing what it is you really want to learn, thereby saving you a lot of time and frustration. Picture the scene. You're having an appraisal interview and agree with your manager that you could do with improving your written reports. She says 'Right, I'll put you down for some communication training'. You may well end up on a three-day course on all aspects of communication, when what you want is to focus specifically on report writing.

Find out time-14

Have you ever been on a training course which left you less than happy at the end of it? I'd be surprised if you haven't.

1   What was the key problem?

2   Did you have a clear idea of what you wanted to achieve *before* you started the course?

3   List some of the objective targets that you'd given yourself.

4 Had you studied the course description and content?

5 Did the course details set out course objectives? (Nowadays, these could be set out as 'competencies' or 'CPD outcomes' – but the intentions are very much the same.)

6 If it did, did you compare these with the objective targets that you'd decided for yourself?

7 If it didn't set out any detailed objectives, etc. why did you bother thinking of attending?

8 Did the course actually meet the objectives it set for itself?

9 If it did – and your objectives matched the course's ones – why are you not happy?

10 How would you change the course content and objectives to meet your needs better?

If you can plan your main objectives or targets, you can compare these with the objectives and targets set out for any particular course or qualification that you're considering (often referred to as programme objectives).

It may help to think in terms of *activities* and *outcomes*. These terms are often used by HR Departments when recording information about your progress. An *activity* is what you do and the *outcome* is the result of what you've done.

It is quite possible for different people to reach the same outcome through different activities.

Take a group of people, with the same outcome required from each of them. The required outcome can be stated as an objective like this:

'By the end of the month, you will be able to describe and discuss the company's Customer First policy, identify the 10 key issues and apply these effectively in a range of monitored events.'

Each individual could potentially learn how to achieve this objective in a different way: courses, private study, coaching and mentoring, learning packages – whichever method turns them on and is available. So although the activities may be different, the target outcome is the same and it's stated clearly in the objective.

Quite often, objectives are referred to as 'CPD Outcomes' or even 'Competency Achievement Levels', but they're all much the same, so don't be put off by the jargon. They're all within the stride of a fine objective thinker like you!

The more you think about what you specifically want to do – and where you specifically want to go – the more confidently and positively you'll be able to get stuck in to your own personal planning. And, if you're enthusiastic about it, it's more likely to happen.

Learning activities

We touched on some of the different ways there are of learning in *Chill out Time 11*.

Some techniques are better for some subjects. You can read about the theory of something like negotiation, for example. But, sooner or later, you'll have to practise doing it. With some subjects, you're probably better discussing different options – in a course group – rather than trying to beaver away on your own.

Some people like doing a course of self-study, usually known as 'open' or 'distance' learning, or, if it's a computerized self-study course, e-learning. Self-study courses allow you to go at your own pace, focus on the areas you find harder to achieve – and basically have a hand in tailoring your own learning. Judge their value against each potential use, however. For example, is an e-learning package really the best way to improve your presentation skills, skills which are highly practical and human-interactive? Packaged learning is great for getting through the theory and structure side of the subject but don't forget the importance of real, practical reinforcement as well.

Computer-based learning has been around in various shapes and sizes for some time now and there's quite a range and choice. When making your selections, focus on the content rather than the medium. Take time to select the programmes which meet your needs and objectives and don't be blinded by technology used for its own sake.

Checking through interactive materials like e-learning programmes or videos does take time. You can scan through a text programme like a workbook fairly quickly and get a feel for whether it meets your needs: is it at the right level and using the right techniques and is the content any good? Where a computerized programme is being sold as having the benefits of interactivity, you'll need to test this by going through it. It's time-consuming but will help you select your best solution.

It helps if you can refer to user reports, written by other learners who have used it. This is something that training departments can often provide.

As well as checking the content and suitability of the material, there's also the computer-use itself. You need to know how to use the technology and programmes before you attempt an e-learning course. E-learning is a new way of learning to many and as with any specific technique, suits some more than others. Once you've learned the techniques, you should be able to use the materials confidently, to best advantage. Give them a try, as this is an obvious way forward for learning, allowing much greater flexibility. The Open University has some good open and e-learning courses with the materials, delivery and support teams set up properly.

Self-study is not necessarily for everyone. Some people prefer or even need the motivation and companionship that a part- or full-time college course provides, while others feel that the content may perhaps have been padded out too much. The advice is the same – shop around. There are enough alternatives now – and more chance of choosing modules you think are relevant – to help you get a mix that suits you, both for content and the amount of time you want to devote to it.

There is a host of similar alternatives to compare and contrast, to review the different ways of learning. Think about them. You do have a choice. Choose ways that suit you – and don't be palmed off with the bog-standard course because it happens to be there. Know where you want to go and you can pick the best route map to get there.

Learning facilities

There are several agencies around that provide information about all the learning and development opportunities around. The website www.learndirect.com (or www.learndirectscotland.com) provided by the University for Industry (Ufl, or SUfl in Scotland) has been set up specifically to bring together details of the different learning events, courses and programmes currently available. Have a look at this or call the helpline (0808 100 9000) to talk through your requirements. Their advisers will talk you through the possible options, using their computerized selection system. They will give you some immediate suggestions of learning providers over the phone and back this up with printouts of course objectives and profiles, so it's a good way of getting started.

There are always a lot of other mentors around – formally or informally – that you can chat with to help sort out your brain and get you heading in the right direction again. Look around – and talk.

The BBC now offers the BBC Learning Zone, which provides programmes in the small hours which you can record for learning use later. The zone covers a vast range of materials – check them out at www.bbc.co.uk/learningzone.

Another detailed list of courses and training on offer can be found at the Department for Education and Skills website – www.dfes.gov.uk.

The local library is also a good place to try, particularly for information on local colleges.

When you start shopping around, you'll find very similar learning programmes available from loads of different sources. There will be courses, packages, self-study programmes and so on, from colleges, commercial companies and local providers like the enterprise/learning & skills councils. What makes one better than another – or one more suitable for your needs? It's down to checking the small print, such as:

- how detailed and precise are the objectives?
- does the programme focus on the study areas you need?
- if it is too detailed, is it possible to select particular bits?
- is it using learning techniques which you like using?
- does it give you help along the way, to keep you progressing?
- is the content well thought out, or is it more spin than substance?
- how closely do the programme objectives match your own?
- is it value for money (even if the money in question is not from your pocket)?
- are there any technical problems you could meet doing the programme?
- what kind of backup support does it give, to help you over hurdles?

The clearer you are in your mind about what you are searching for – the easier it will be to know when you've found it.

Learning resources

If you're a sheep person, working in a business gives you an extra benefit. As well as having the options on the open market, you should also be able to call on learning support from the company itself. However, the supply of training within companies seems to wax and wane quite a lot with a tendency for learning/training to suffer when budgets become tight.

That's often the time when some of those informal methods of learning from other people, e.g. coaching and mentoring which we mentioned at the beginning of this chapter, are seen as more desirable.

Chill out time-12

Think of the situation as a triangle, with you at one corner and the mentor/coach/buddy at the second corner, working away happily, with you learning something new.

Wait. You're right – triangles have three corners.

So, what else do we need to get balanced progress?

You need backup and support from Training – or let's call them the 'Development Support Function'.

Think about the types of support which will be useful.

The idea of a triangle is a powerful one, if you think about it. It's the:

- trinity
- the strengthening support in a gate
- a method of measuring accurately
- the simplest form of interaction.

Here's something to try.

Work out time-17

Find an elastic band.

Using your thumb and first two fingers as the three corner points of a triangle, slip the elastic band round their tips to make your triangle.

Move your fingers and thumb around a little, changing the shape of the triangle.

Notice how the relationship between the three points changes – with closer bonds between one pair at one time and between another a moment later. In each case, the third point remains there, supporting and interacting, keeping some form of bonded triangle in place. That's the bonding role of the triangle – the trinity.

Think of the learning triangle: sometimes you will be the individual learner; sometimes you will be the coach/mentor. You might even be involved in providing the resource support. You could be any one of the three roles, at any given moment.

As these roles change, think of the triangle revolving, like a Catherine Wheel firework. That's 360° mentoring. Think of the energy that's being generated.

Now, slip the elastic band off your first finger. Your thumb and second finger will be working directly against each other. Action and reaction – the synergy's lost.

Think about it.

So – sheep types can get support from within their organization, as well as from outside. Perhaps goat types have to search around a bit more, know where to look – and do more of the looking themselves – but there's plenty for them as well. In some cases, there will be opportunities which are only open to a particular type of goats – the self-employed, the unemployed or people from particular groups or types. Keep asking around, the details are out there.

If you're thinking about pursuing some learning yourself (whether you're in a sheep or a goat situation), bear in mind that you can apply for financial support through the Individual Learning Account scheme. You can get details of this through learndirect as well.

Find out time-15

1   What are the key reference sources I can call on in my area?

2   How can I go about tapping in to free or subsidized learning and development?

3   What are some of the high priority issues I have personally?

4   How do these tie in with the priorities which my employer or clients have?

5   Compromising if necessary, which priorities should I focus on?

6   What do I want/need to do first?

7 Can I write that fairly tightly as an objective or outcome statement? Yes/No

8 If the answer to 7 was *Yes*, have a go at doing it. If *No*, read the last few pages once more, then ask yourself the question again. You can do it, sure you can.

9 What measures will I set myself to judge when I've achieved the outcome?

10 Who can I call upon to help me along the way, if necessary?

11 What do I have to set up, so that I can get going?

Bite sized chunks

We spoke about this earlier. Keep the image in front of you. It'll stop you trying to run before you can crawl and keep you from overloading on too much information, without having the chance to practise it. The idea has lots of different applications:

■ learning in small sections

■ seeing the chunks as progressive building blocks

■ understanding the importance of regular review, or consolidation

■ helping the mentor/coach and learner work together positively

■ focusing on the expected outcome of each chunk

■ selecting the chunks that are really relevant to your needs.

It helps you get things into perspective – and feel on top of them. Then, if the worst comes to the worst, you know how to be selective, you know where your priorities lie, so that you can keep your head above water.

Work/life balance

Returning to the question posed by the title of this chapter – How do I advance? – your answer will depend in part on how you feel about your current work/life balance. Use this exercise to check it out.

Chill out time-13

This is important, so try and find a quiet spot so you can spend 15 or so minutes thinking without fear of interruption.

- Do you feel you're spending enough time with your immediate family – or 'significant others'?

- Are you proud of the number of hours you spend at work, if you're a sheep person, or the number of e-mails you receive each day, if you're a goat person?

- Is it smart working very long hours? Is your effectiveness suffering?

- Is there any way you can control your time better?

- Would working part-time or job-sharing be a possible option for you?

- Is there any way you could reduce your monthly expenses, to relieve pressures?

- How would you spend more time on your life, on living?

It really is worth asking yourself sometimes: 'Do I really want to be doing that?'

Don't be impressed by the 'jacket on the back of the chair' syn-drome – the people that apparently work long into the evening, because they're so important or they're proud of 'holding down a high flying job'. It's the outcomes that are important in life, more so than the activities. Work smart and you can reach the outcome with the least possible effort, in the least possible time.

In a survey conducted by the Chartered Institute of Personnel and Development, one of the conclusions was that 'although 75% wished that their partners worked fewer hours, 65% would not want their partner to get a new job if it meant a cut in the household budget'. There isn't a lot of hope for individuals sorting out their work/life bal-ance if their 'significant other' is happy seeing less of them as long as the money keeps rolling in.

Planning for your brilliant future should take work/life balances into account. If you're thinking holistically – and you are by now, aren't you! – you'll see that there's more to it than the number of hours you work per week. You have to think about:

- identifying life skills you can apply at work – and vice versa
- being able to focus on each in turn – without allowing 'interfer-ence' to distract
- making best use of quality time, for both work and life subdivisions
- maintaining a healthy balance – not burning the candle at both ends
- leaving any negative work baggage in the workplace – and vice versa.

Thinking objectively will help you make these kinds of decisions and allow you to cope better with the stresses and strains of both work and life. It's got to be flexible though. There will be times where you might have to work longer for a few days when a new project is coming on stream. Equally, there might be times when you need a bit more Life-time, for example, when a child is ill.

A company which will regularly expect the former, while bearing down remorselessly on the latter is frankly not worth working for, if that's their official company policy. If instead, it boils down to being the short-sighted attitudes of one inflexible manager, well then, there's perhaps more you can do about it, to rebalance your own work/life equilibrium. Objective thinking and win/win negotiation can save the day.

So, how does this work/life thinking affect your planning?

Find out **time-16**

1 Is study/development time going to eat into my home life?

2 If so, is it going to do so in the short term or the long term? Is that acceptable to everyone concerned?

3 What life skills do I have which are useful at work? Can I develop these further?

4 What time-wasting things at work can I reduce – or get rid of completely?

5 Are others' activities (or lack of them) affecting how I spend my time at work?

6 How would I really want to spend my non-work time? Can I do this?

7 Am I regularly too tired to do the things I want to do – and should be doing – at home?

8 How can I start to organize my work/life balance better?

9 How would I write these as objective statements, each beginning with an action verb?

10 How do my personal and my professional development priorities stack up together?

You've been focusing on your key objectives and the range of opportunities which you can call on to progress further along your path. If you are a sheep within a company structure, how do you best work within the existing formats of the company?

With a bit of objective planning and clear thinking, you can finish up going to your boss with a fairly precise 'shopping list' of what you want to do, with detailed explanations of what and why – and even how. Well, OK, maybe some of your suggestions will still be a bit hesitant but you're certainly getting there.

Dealing with disappointment

What happens when your boss says no?

This needs objective, bigger picture thinking too. Picture all the individual learning paths snaking along the main track once more. Each of these paths – and the little glimmer of energy at the head of it – needs assistance and input. Some more than others. You are but one of these glimmers of energy. Your boss – and other bosses – are responsible for the whole constellation. So, see yourself in proportion.

It doesn't mean you give up, or flounce off in a tantrum because you're not getting the support you think you deserve. It means you reassess your priorities. Not just within your own guidelines, but within the priorities and needs of the department and company you're working in. You may not even be aware of some of the future departmental plans, requiring particular skills, for example. So listen for the detail and take it on board. Show yourself to be a flexible, co-operative thinker (without being weak, of course) and you gain brownie points. Because you've managed to state and describe your needs and priorities clearly, opportunities which link in with these are more likely to come with your name written on them.

The waiting can be frustrating, but awareness and acceptance of the need for waiting is more than half the battle.

Work out time-18

There's a saying:

'You are what you want to be.'

Certainly true, however, you're not just waiting for luck to play a part. If you're focused, you can help make things happen – in time.

Notice, the saying doesn't include 'when you want to be it' – but the waiting improves the final achievement.

Think of one of your development needs.

Think of the 'best scenario' target – when you'd ideally need to be able to do it.

Think realistically of the 'worst scenario' – when you would be having problems if you couldn't do that particular thing properly, due to lack of knowledge or skill.

That gives you your guidelines to work and negotiate between.

So, you won't always get the go-ahead to do all the development you want. Who knows, there will be situations where delays will help you change your needs to meet new situations. There's usually a rainbow in there amongst the clouds somewhere!

The timing and flexibility applies if you're a goat as well. Delays to your development plans could be caused by:

- budget or grant restrictions
- time pressures to keep your business going
- availability of public events without expensive travel and accommodation
- availability of commercial programmes that really meet your needs
- lack of internal colleagues to act as support.

There's invariably a bigger picture out there. Think of the mass of intertwining paths again. That's the development picture, with you as one of the glimmers of energy.

Chill out time-14

Visualize these paths, each with its energy source.

You are one of these individual energy sources.

See how the paths cross each other, sometimes running parallel and supportive, sometimes getting in each other's way, sometimes meandering, sometimes travelling straight and fast.

Each individual needs support, sometimes a lot, sometimes very little.

What is your present direction? What are your present needs?

How do they fit in with the needs and priorities of others?

How do you make them happen?

What timescale will be possible?

In some ways, as a goat, you may find it harder to locate support, but then, when you do, you're probably in a better position to do what you want. Bigger picture thinking will help you rationalize. It can be a bit lonely out there as a goat, sometimes, without the backup and support you might prefer. There are associations, business clubs, professional institutes and so on that you can belong to, as well as local and national reference sources you can contact. Look around you – you have friends and contacts out there.

Once you're clearer about your needs and priorities – through objective thinking – you will be able to sort out the way forward. The *ID Plan* system will help you do that.

It's time to have a closer look at this, and how it can support your brilliant future planning.

7 Recording my progress

So, let's see where we've got to along your development path.

You've been considering your needs, priorities, current status and so on in some detail, through the range of different exercises you've completed so far. As we reconsider some of this with a more structured planning system in mind, you may have to check back to remind yourself of some of the brilliant ideas you had at the time.

Using a planning system

What we need to do now is get some order into the planning. We also have to sort out some form of consistent structure to use. You'll be reviewing a whole range of development activities, so you'll need to have a sequence of steps and stages which you're happy using for each one. Using this sequence of formats for planning each priority, you'll build up a set of checklists which relate to each individual activity. You soon get into the way of using the formats which you've selected as relevant to your needs. Doing this, you'll build up parallel sets of planning references for each of your development activities. It all gradually becomes easier – and faster. That way, you can see the benefits of using a system to note the checks, balances and information, preventing it from all appearing to be an administrative nightmare.

The important thing with any planning system – and especially one which needs you to put in a fair amount of effort completing it – is that you, the user, think it's worth completing properly. Not just for a week or so while the enthusiasm's still there – but over a longer period. For that to happen, you need to:

- use formats and fields which seem relevant to each specific need
- complete them only in enough detail to be useful, rather than tedious
- feel that the structure is helping you plan your development consistently
- believe that it is relevant to your particular (sheep/goat) work situation
- write using objective language, to allow cross-reference with business priorities.

Perhaps you've had experience of using some form of diary planning system and even carry one around with you. If you do, it's likely that you use some of these format pages more than others, as you've found through experience that these are the ones which are more relevant. After all, the system's there as a support, not a hindrance. The same is true for any development planner. Think of it as a combined memory jogger and information store. What information do you think is worth storing? Focus on your personal development needs closely for a moment. Make notes for future reference.

Find out time-17

1   What information do you need to know about yourself in order to plan your future development?

2   How can you sort out your development priorities?

3 What techniques can you use to link your personal development priorities with your work needs and priorities? How can you identify and respond to any blockages?

4 What can you do to check whether you're heading in the right direction?

5 How can you get a consistent pattern working for each of your development priority areas?

6 What information do you need in order to set up this consistent pattern?

7 How do you link your personal development plans and actions with your working needs?

8 Where can you find the support and assistance to make all this happen effectively?

9 How do you sort out any blockages, keep an eye on progress and record it precisely?

10 How can you link your personal development in an open way with the 'bigger picture'?

---

11 What form of action planning can you use to monitor your short- and longer-term progress?

There's lots to think about there.

Some sections of it will seem more important to you than others. That's fine. Your responses and priorities will vary in line with where you are along your own personal development path.

Despite this flexibility and variety however, you do need to think in an ordered, logical way, to some greater or lesser extent. It helps you to plan over a longer period of time. It also helps when you're trying to relate different specific areas to the bigger picture of your overall development. And it helps within an organization or business of any type, when you're trying to position your development alongside that of others – and the future direction of the business itself. Brilliant futures don't just happen – they need consistent help along the way. It can come in different shapes and sizes and you can apply it in a variety of ways but one way or another, an overall structure is not only useful but very necessary to assist positive progress.

Organizing the information

Think of that personal organizer diary system again. Whichever type you use, somewhere in there will be the daily action plan/'things to do' list type of format page. In its simplest form, the 'things to do' list is almost a blank sheet of paper. The back of an old envelope would do just as well – for many people, it does! It works with this activity because we know what we're doing. It's a means of personal brainstorming, of getting our ideas, thoughts, concerns, plans – anything that could be relevant to our future development needs – down on paper.

Using this type of information logging, it becomes much easier to sort out priorities, eliminate the occasional idea which just won't work when considered logically and review the detail necessary to get you moving. And, at the other end of the activity, it becomes immensely satisfying when you can check back to your list periodically and tick off or score out the actions which you've completed. That's motivation for you.

So, at the one extreme of personal organizer formats, you have what is virtually a blank sheet of paper, which is still very valuable. At the other extreme, you find quite complex sequences of responses required, set down within impressive layouts, e.g. project management reports or financial planning schemes. The more detailed response cues in these formats make sure you think consistently each time you use them and make sure that you're providing the type and amount of information necessary to link in with other systems or users. Through practice, you'll doubtless develop your own way of adapting and completing them. Having sorted out your own particular method of use, it's likely that you tend towards completing each format using similar techniques each time. This speeds things up, eases any necessary cross-reference and helps others who have to work alongside you as well, of course.

It's this level of consistency, structure and cross-reference which we find in the personal organizer that we want to set up for your personal and professional development as well. Through the exercises which you've completed so far in this book you've already thought through many of these important prompt questions.

At this stage in our progress, we need to get a range of formats sorted out which you will find useful. You have already begun to crystallize this range in the previous FIND OUT exercise you completed. Now it's time to focus some more.

Work out time-19

You've already considered at various stages whether you tend towards being a sheep or a goat as far as work practices and environment are concerned.

You've set down some of the priorities and considered the types of responses and research that you'll need to do, to set your brilliant sheep or goat future in progress.

So, straight away, there will be some branched routes to select on your development path, when you reach each junction signpost saying 'sheep thinkers this way/goat thinkers that way'.

Here's a chance to practise thinking objectively. Think of a sequence of personal development planning, which will give you the steps and stages which you may need to chart your own development path.

As a start point, let me offer you a sequence of milestones, to see how these might fit your own particular intended journey.

Milestone 1 Where do I stand just now?

Milestone 2 How do I sort out my priorities?

Milestone 3 How can I respond best to develop my key priorities?

Milestone 4 What support can I call on to help this development?

Milestone 5 Can I predict potential blocks – and if so, how can I overcome them?

Milestone 6 How can I check/confirm that I'm heading in the best direction?

Milestone   7 What detail do I need to focus on each of my development needs?

Milestone   8 How do I link this information with details of organized learning plans?

Milestone 9 What techniques can I use to make sure I'm thinking objectively?

Milestone 10 What detail do I need to write an action plan to develop this need?

Milestone 11 How can I check whether this personal plan fits the 'bigger picture'?

Milestone 12 Reviewing these last few milestones, is any revision necessary?

Milestone 13 Which ways and techniques of learning would I prefer to use here?

Milestone 14 How do I manage to obtain the support I need?

Milestone 15 What can I do to log progress and keep my path moving positively?

Milestone 16 What detail do I have to provide for any formal recording systems?

Milestone 17 Does this requirement alter my priorities in any way? If so, how?

Milestone 18 How does this development area influence my work/life balance?

Milestone 19 How can I get more involved in the development areas of others?

Milestone 20 At this moment, what are my key present and future 'things to do'?

How does that sequence seem to you? There's a definite logic to it, which I have applied with lots of people on seminars – but it's my logic and that doesn't necessarily fit yours! There is potential for flexibility, so not to worry.

If it's a case of seeing greater value in some milestones than others, that's certainly not a problem. You may even find that priorities will shift depending on the particular development area you're considering at the moment. It's important that you see this way of thinking generally as a help rather than a hindrance. So just use the milestones and ways of thinking that you find comfortable and useful. Sometimes, you may feel like adapting some ideas, so that they fit your own way of thinking better. It's usually easier to improve upon the design of a wheel than to come up with the original concept. Respond as your needs dictate.

You might agree with the questions but consider it more logical to ask them in a different sequence of milestones. That doesn't really matter. Just alter the numbers appropriately on the formats, as required, if you feel more comfortable considering the issues in a different sequence.

The sequence which is indicated in the series of milestones in that previous exercise is one that progresses gradually from analysing the current status, through monitoring progress and general direction, to finally recording progress and relating this to the 'bigger picture'. This thinking uses the same thought processes which were used to develop the sequence of *ID Plan* formats which form an integral part of this book.

The *ID Plan*

If you're reading this book as a result of accessing the *ID Plan* format pages on the *www.business-minds.com* website, you'll already be aware of their existence and are now, I hope, finding out more about the thinking behind them and their applications.

If you're reading the book first, without having experienced the web-based format pages, you may have already picked up my references to the use of a planning system. The web-based *ID Plan* format pages are the integrated planning elements of this system. We'll be progressing through the specific steps and stages of completing them in Chapter 10, so we shouldn't be focusing on the detail yet.

At this point in the process, we need to confirm that all /most/ some of the proposed format pages meet your individual development needs. We're focusing on the principle behind the formats and their overall purpose and application. The key question is – can you buy into the general idea?

It's time to have a general look at the *ID Plan* format pages, if you haven't already done this. You'll find them on the website *www. business-minds.com*, or there are reduced versions in the appendix of this book. Remember, we're not bothered about the detail contained in the format pages at this stage – we're more interested in seeing how the logic flows between formats and whether they cover the areas you feel you need to consider. And, if you can accept the logic, you then want to ask yourself whether the sequence makes sense to your way of planning your brilliant future.

Find out time-18

1 Looking back at the sequence of milestones in the previous Work Out exercise, are you generally comfortable with this form and sequence of thinking?

2 Are there any milestones which you'd rather not pause at – or even reach in the first place? If there are, make a note of them, with a reason why each is not appropriate to your needs.

3 Are there any areas of individual planning and priorities which come to mind, which seem important to you but are not included in the milestone sequence? If so, make a note of them.

4 Comparing and contrasting the flow and sequence (not the detailed content at this stage) of the different *ID Plan* format pages, can you follow a cross-relationship between these and the sequence of Milestones in *WORK OUT Time 19* This may take some time to do but it will help to reinforce the flow.

5 Looking at the Sheep/Goat parallels in Formats 3/4 and 8/9, can you identify which is more appropriate to your need and see the parallels in the questions, comparing each pair?

6 If you are aware of any formal recording of training and development detail within your work environment, how would some of these format pages be valuable in relation to these current systems?

7 Looking at the format pages generally, do you feel positive about the thought of using them to help direct your planning – or do you feel your heart sinking at the whole idea?

8 If you do have concerns, is there anything positive you can do to make the system more usable for your particular needs?

9 At a glance, do some format pages seem more interesting than others? If this is the case, can you figure out why? Does this indicate any changes to be made which would help you?

---

10 Have you ever thought about your personal development in this way before?

As a result of this consolidation and review and with an overall awareness of the types of format pages you will be using to chart your brilliant future, I hope that you are full of ideas and positive thoughts. You can control your own way forward; you can get directly involved in your own learning and development; you can be an active party in designing your own career path and broadening your outlook to life.

We have provided an open-ended format page matrix within the *ID Plan* system, which you can use to create any additional formats you require to suit your needs.

Chill out **time-15**

Reviewing any type of form which requires completion can be rather daunting.

Many are rather 'official', e.g. tax forms or the census and may include requests for information which you'd rather not give.

ID Plan is special to you. It's giving you a focus to think of information and plan strategies which will help you develop. So, if there's any information you don't think is relevant – or which you don't want to think about – you *don't have to*. No penalties. No threats or fines. You are in control.

It also allows you the flexibility to complete it as you see fit and to add additional sections, if you see these as being valuable. You are in control.

Picture your way ahead as a series of milestones heading off into the distance.

These milestones are there to help and encourage you to progress.

View them positively – stay and ponder some.

For others, use them as a guide but move smartly and rapidly on to the next one.

This is your development path. This is your life. You are in control.

Summary

Planning and recording your progress in an ordered way is a valuable activity. It:

- gives you a structure to follow, encouraging consistency
- makes sure that you include all the relevant detail
- encourages objective thinking
- helps you relate your development to that of others and your business
- indicates recap points, to help you check on your progress
- helps to highlight blocks before they become crises – to allow remedial action
- allows you to keep control over your priorities and progress.

We need some time at this stage to consolidate the ideas. You may need to get your head round the whole idea of committing your future plans to paper. Within a fairly bureaucratic world, we might need time to see the value of applying a self-created bureaucratic system. You will need to think through the different logics represented in the sequences and see whether you can accept the general principle of my suggested system.

So, let's leave the whole *I D Plan* concept on hold for the moment – although you will be continuing to think about it subconsciously – and return to some techniques to apply when reviewing your brilliant future.

part three

broaden
your
scope

This section helps you see the bigger picture – to think more holistically, so that you can achieve results which are greater than the sum of the individual efforts made. It contains ideas and tips, to expand your personal and professional development techniques.

8 Applying the brain – the way ahead

There are many theories around when it comes to studying the brain. I'm not intending to expand on any of them here – there are lots of books written by specialists in mind mapping, neuro linguistic programming (NLP) and similar techniques. Have a look at these if you're interested – it's always better getting the information from the original sources.

What I'd like to focus on in this chapter is how we can best use our brains – or perhaps more specifically, our minds – to view the world in a broader way, thinking 'big picture'. I don't want to get into any deep discussions, medical or metaphysical, about the difference between brains and minds. I am using the word 'mind' to mean attitudes, concepts, beliefs, awareness and all the myriad of other mental activities and outcomes which can happen, if we allow them. The brain, on the other hand, is that corrugated melon that you see in pictures – a physical thing responsible for driving different parts of our bodies. It's the infinite computer that drives our more visible bits. So here, we're thinking of mind in the broader way implied by the 'mind, body and spirit' concept rather than brain in 'brainpower'.

Logic and creativity

Having said that, let's start by focusing on thinking, as it's normally physically linked with parts of the brain. You've probably heard the expression 'left brain/right brain thinking'. Left brain involves your more logical thoughts, while right brain thinking is more creative. The disorganized, scatty artist or musician is immediately considered to be, obviously, a right brain thinker. Pedantic, humourless accountant – self-evident – he's a left brain thinker.

There is talk in training texts and seminars about whether you are a left or a right brain thinker and compartmentalizing individuals as right or left brain types is often taken as the reason or excuse for the ways people act and exist. Once again, as with considering learning or individual/team styles, this approach can appear over-simplistic. We are in the main too complex to be considered merely one or the other, or even strongly biased towards one aspect for all decision making. Can you have a creative, logical thinker? A right/left brain thinker? Of course you can. The world of architecture must encourage the breed – producing individuals who can follow all the design and technical requirements logically but still create a building of imagination and beauty.

We are attempting to combine right and left brain thinking in our brilliant future activities as well, when we're trying to apply open, co-operative ideas within a work environment. It's often hard finding the right balance for this combination. A gross generalization is that business thinking probably tends towards the logical or left brain. We apply more of this left brain involvement at the assertive level of ordered business activity – with a greater use of the creative, right brain thinking when we attempt to incorporate more co-operative or dynamic principles. Perhaps one of the secret ingredients which gives an entrepreneur the edge over others is an ability to think creatively – and laterally. There is also an element of luck involved, in creating something which can be sold on at vast profit but the vision needs to be there initially.

So, as with our architects' style, if we're attempting to apply holistic thinking within business, we are also combining left and right brain thinking. In our planning for a brilliant future, we're trying to apply a logical sequence within our development plans, to help us flourish dynamically and creatively. Putting it another way, we're using objective thinking to plan and share co-operative ideas with our buddies and team mates, in order to get dynamic and creative outcomes.

It's an obvious goal, but the results, however achieved, really give you the old whoopee feeling again. Linking individual with team development gives us that extra something – the added benefit of working with others which we miss when flying solo. The outcome becomes worth more than the sum of the individual inputs. It's that team thing! We have the secret added ingredient.

Thinking holistically

Work out time-20

Take a simple example, which we've already touched on in an earlier exercise.

Think of a group of four individuals doing some form of group activity – giving a group presentation, carrying out an oil drum raft construction exercise or reviewing current working practices in the department, for example.

Each individual will have particular skills. Mix these skills together and you get an extra dynamic – it's called synergy sometimes – which produces an effect and result which is better than you could expect from any one of the four carrying out the same exercise. The end result is worth more than the sum of the parts. This, as you now know, is the holistic effect.

With properly structured personal development, we can look for similar results (or outcomes) from an individual's efforts. We're thinking further than merely taking management development training as separate elements. We're considering how the act of applying the skills we already have in one area to enhance our skills in another can give improved spin-off results. We're trying to measure how these development elements affect and integrate with each other and what added benefits this can bring. Such as:

- can you communicate more clearly when negotiating?
- will your work prioritization help you delegate to others more sensibly?
- does your knowledge of work practices help you understand others' needs?
- can you apply objective thinking to help others as well as yourself to progress?

- can you give the time to mentor and coach others?
- how can you use your financial and business knowledge to explain future plans?

These activities – and others which you can doubtless think of which fit your own work/life environment – are all incorporating different skills and knowledge areas to make you more capable or competent overall. Some are applying your 'life skills' at work, while others give you a chance to use work skills to help you live a fuller and better life, to make you a 'better person' – but not in a 'goody, goody' way. More a broader, more thoughtful person – using more of your mind, in a more mindful way. So, you're no longer thinking in terms of learning new skills or techniques in little compartments, to apply as self-contained efforts. Instead, you're trying to see how you can cross-fertilize these skills, to gain overall, improved results.

Lateral thinking

Isn't it wonderful sometimes when there's a group of people discussing something and, all of a sudden, one of the party makes a statement which stops everyone dead in their tracks. Everyone's been thinking down a particular avenue and, flash, someone shines a torch down an alleyway which is off at a tangent from the main route. The immediate reaction is 'What on earth's that got to do with what we're talking about?', followed in rapid succession with 'Of course, that's quite possible, if we look at it from that angle!'

We need to apply lateral thinking when we're thinking about ways of learning. To some people, learning means attending a course, full stop. No debate. That's the way it's always been and will continue to be.

Presenting a range of options, with ideas of best practice for each, can be seen as a real lateral thinking challenge by some, with different people needing to put in varying levels of effort in order to make this initial shift. Never lose sight of the fact that it's really hard for some people to change perspective so fundamentally, although it may just seem like common sense to others. Co-operation requires patience.

Some professionals champion one technique, be it course learning, computer-based learning, action-centred learning or whatever. Like the old philosophers who maintained that the earth was flat and borne on the backs of elephants, once they've nailed their colours to the mast with a particular and unique belief, it's hard to accept the alternative proposals of others. Many out-of-date scientific theories are kept alive by such pundits, who would lose the reason for their existence and past 30 years of research if they accepted that their policies or research results were open to debate.

In many of the exercises so far, you have been recording your immediate responses, in the hope of getting to your true feelings and beliefs. Don't think too deeply and long. Don't try and figure out what the 'correct/expected' answer would be. Go with the flow. That's what brainstorming is trying to achieve. That's where you're tending towards using the right side of your brain to get that creativity flowing. That's when lateral thinking is more likely to happen.

Try this.

Work out time-21

1   What do you really want to do – now?

2   What's stopping you doing it?

3   Is that a real issue?

4   How could you get round that problem – if indeed it is a problem?

5   How else could you start doing what you want to do?

6   Are there any extra things you'll have to do, to compensate?

7   Now, can you do what you really want to do?

8   Do you really want to do it?

9   Do it!

I believe it's valuable to spend some time thinking through possible options combining objective and lateral thinking, to prepare yourself for situations which might happen in the future. This then puts you in a position to respond more quickly when you do come up against these kinds of situations because your brain kicks in with a range of options and ideas. Call it prior planning, lateral thinking or whatever – but it helps come up with solutions fast. You can react more immediately, in a more creative way, because you've planned the detail through logically beforehand. You've used planning and logic to assist creativity. The left brain has helped the right brain towards a better final result. Some might see us as spontaneous lateral thinkers but prior planning has helped.

It's the same with seeing the 'bigger picture'. How big is your normal take on the world?

Find out time-19

1   What's the key international news issue just now?

_____

2   How long has it been going on, in its present form?

_____

3   How have these events developed/changed recently?

_____

4   When did you last travel further than 30 miles from your home and/or place of work?

_____

5 Are you aware of local issues which are seen differently by others living elsewhere?

6 Have you ever complained publicly about an issue which affects others more than you?

7 Do you get involved in community activities which may not benefit you directly?

8 Can you identify actions which will have a greater effect on society, long-term?

9 Do you accept news at face value or do the personalized angles and 'spin' annoy you?

10 What have you done recently which might just make the world a better place?

Seeing the bigger picture

Viewing the bigger picture involves stepping back, thinking things through from different angles and considering the effects which actions and decisions might have on a scale which is larger than your normal perspective.

This in itself gives us a vast range, depending on each person's normal vista. Have you ever seen the scenario where someone has returned to their car and is obviously going to vacate their parking space? Another car hovers, waiting for the car to leave but the first driver fiddles around for ages, either totally oblivious to the fact that someone is waiting or perhaps completerly unconcerned by their needs?

In villages – and, indeed, in localized urban areas or 'manors' – we often find a narrow, parochial style of thinking where people can't see past the events of their own direct surroundings. They may well be fully aware of what's happening in their favourite TV soap – but have little idea of what's going on in the world. Bigger picture thinking, taken generally, is thus a progressive thing; it depends initially on the size and range of the person's current awareness. Start by looking beyond personal needs and local priorities.

Seeing the actions of the world from a very narrow, localized perspective in this way is a common problem. It makes seeing the bigger picture quite hard for some. When you're planning your future, for example, we've established that you need to tie in your needs with the priorities of the business and others. Logic states that you're more likely to get the support you want if you can co-operate with others to some extent. This does not prevent some demanding their rights and generally ruffling feathers to get their own way regardless.

You too will be involved with the bigger picture when you're planning your own brilliant future by:

- linking your progress with that of others and the needs of your work

- seeing how your needs can adapt to fit with more widespread needs and vice versa, to get the best mix

- building your own priorities so that they marry with those of others, to give you the best support for what you want to do

- planning how you can help others so that the atmosphere's right for others to help you

■ comparing your milestones with those of others, to see beyond possible blocks and delays.

They're all examples of viewing your future in a more objective way.

When you're thinking about ways of learning new skills or areas of knowledge, you're more likely to find a range of good materials – or variety of worthwhile learning events – when you're dealing with the more popular subject areas. So, thinking objectively, you're more likely to be able to 'pick and mix' to suit your own personal needs and priorities. Use awareness of the bigger picture to map out your most valuable path along the track.

When you're arguing a case from the bigger perspective, it gives you more scope and evidence, but make sure you're 'singing from the same hymnsheet' as your listeners. Don't assume they can follow the argument from this broader viewpoint (or indeed that they are aware of what the broader perspective is). There is still a fair amount of subjectivity – and parochialism – around. Explain what you mean. Assume nothing (which doesn't mean boring your audience into the ground with detail – merely checking that they're following what you're saying).

Stress

There's a lot of talk about stress nowadays. A little stress is quite healthy – it keeps you on your toes and, in a mild, non-aggressive way, encourages fight rather than flight. It gets you out of bed and off to work in the mornings; it drives you to persevere so that you meet your goals and gain the satisfaction of success. We're thinking of higher levels of stress here, where it can seriously disrupt your ability to work effectively.

Stress at this more persistent level is often caused by others so working smarter will not necessarily release you from stress – unless you learn how to say 'No' politely. However, also remember that your actions can cause stress in others, if you don't think co-operatively. That last-minute request for a letter or report; that lack of decision-making and direction on your part which leaves others to sort out problems and make decisions which are really your responsibility. Delegation – good thing; passing the buck – *big* stress maker for others!

So, how can we overcome stress to focus our minds to relax and find that inner calm? This is a study all on its own but let's just spend a moment or two sampling one or two techniques.

When trying to see the bigger picture or plan ahead, it's often quite hard to cut out the distractions which are all around us. Open plan offices, 'my door is always open' policies and the general atmosphere of movement and interruptions all add up to a heap of interference to the potential progress of our thoughts. We speak about 'trains of thought'. It often takes some time to get on board that train, and one interruption can set you back many stations, until you remember where you were – if you can. Try this.

Chill out time-16

This activity is good for helping you shut out distractions and concentrate on something which you consider to be important for an acceptable period of time.

There's so much going on around you that the mind finds it very difficult to lock onto one unique thought for any length of time. We're probably not even talking minutes here – you're doing well if you can really focus on a single thought for one minute, initially.

Try it, if you don't believe me!

This is mind focusing – or meditation, if you're comfortable with that expression. You don't have to sign away your soul or anything – just go with the flow. Like many such exercises, finding the time to do it is half the solution. Focusing your mind on something, in a pleasant, disturbance-free atmosphere, will allow you to switch off from the hubbub of the world. That in itself will reduce your stress levels. It's certainly worth a try.

Find yourself a quiet room where you can settle down comfortably somewhere. Put on some quiet music, if that helps cut out distractions – nothing with singing or other forms of distracting words. You're better sitting upright on a chair, stool or the floor, if you prefer. Rest your hands on your thighs, or hold them comfortably in front of you. Keep your back straight.

With your eyes closed, concentrate for a while on your breathing. Breathe slowly and deeply: breathe out; pause; breathe in; pause. When you focus on it, you'll probably be quite surprised at how shallow your normal breathing is, when you compare it. Continue to focus on your breathing. Slowly breathe in ... and out.

Now, think of three related thoughts which you can focus on. They could be:

- three places around the world which need some help – for war, drought or whatever
- three people you know who are ill and need healing and positive thoughts
- three activities which you need to do to help others, or achieve a goal
- three local areas which need improvement – to make them better environments.

That kind of thing. Any group of ideas which are important to you, but to others as well.

Once you've thought of these, you need to switch from focusing on your breathing to thinking about the first thought. Thinking about it in a positive way. Thinking about how it could be improved, helped, made better in some way. You will find your mind beginning to stray after some time. In the early stages, this period of time may well be very short. That's OK.

As soon as you find your mind wandering from Thought 1, move on to focus on Thought 2. And so on, moving back to Thought 1 and continue in the circle of thoughts. Don't allow yourself to think about anything else – if you want a break, concentrate deeply on your breathing again, before focusing back on one of your thoughts.

Carry on for as long as you feel comfortable. For the first few times, 5–10 minutes is probably long enough. As your mind focus ability develops, you can go for longer – perhaps 20 minutes or half an hour. It's the depth of concentration you're trying to achieve that's important, not the length of time. If you find yourself planning what you need to buy at the supermarket or figuring out how you're going to construct that set of shelves, you're 'off message', as the politicians would say.

So, when you begin to feel that you've focused on your three thoughts as long as comfortably possible, focus on your breathing for one last session and gradually speed up your breathing until you come back into the world of bustle and myriad thoughts.

You should feel more relaxed as a result and have gained the benefit of clearer thoughts on your chosen subject. That's the power of meditation.

There are, of course, lots of different forms of meditation. This one concentrates on focusing the mind on specific ideas, with the result that other extraneous ideas are shut out. With other forms, the purpose is to vacate the mind completely by using sounds or repeated words (mantras) to focus on. Some take you into a much deeper level of concentration. We'll just stick with this for the moment, as we're more concerned with the benefits of focusing our minds to allow more brilliant planning – for our more brilliant future.

Visualization

There's a spin-off which you can also try, which again helps you to cope with stress when things are not going well. You can use it when you've come up against a block, perhaps, or when timescales are getting out of hand. It's not there to help you figure out work problems or help the world. Called visualization, it's a method of giving you respite – a bit of pleasure and relaxation, so that you can then face up to the world again as a more confident, relaxed person. It can help prevent you collapsing as a quaking heap on the floor in times of stress – so that can't be bad either!

Visualization works best when it's led by someone talking you through the stages. This one is just for you to try yourself, so is very much a 'taster'.

Chill out time-17

Get yourself in the comfortable position again as described in Chill Out 16. You can use appropriate sounds effects e.g. woodland, beach and sea sounds rather than music, if you have them.

As you get more used to the idea, you can use your imagination and create new scenes for yourself but, at this early stage, it's easier to imagine a scene you have already experienced. A walk in a wood or by a river; a walk along a lonely beach shoreline; lying somewhere pleasant with the sun on your face. Whatever turns on your whoopee button.

So, once you've decided what your location and scene is, you need to picture yourself in the scene. Imagine yourself doing specific things, looking around, seeing and smelling things. Hear the noises which are going on around you – but focus on the pleasant ones. The sounds of the water, the wind, birdsong, anything which helps to create the scene in detail in your mind.

As your enjoyment and concentration on the scene increases, breathe more slowly and deeply. Enjoy the benefits of the scene: the peace; the warmth; the fact of being on your own, or with people whose company you enjoy. Pick some fruit to eat, or imagine yourself eating something which you appreciate.

If you feel like it, imagine yourself moving around in the scene, doing things which help you relax.

Carry on this whole scene for as long as you need to give you some degree of relaxation and use the same breathing technique to gradually bring yourself back to your usual world. But, even then, give yourself time to phase back in. Don't go rushing off to 'make up for lost time'. It hasn't been 'lost' time – it's been quality time to maintain your sanity, balance and ability to make rational decisions. So – enjoy it and don't feel guilty in any way.

Have a short break; sit and gather your thoughts. Do whatever is necessary to gently bring yourself back to thinking about the work in hand, in a more rational, relaxed way, stage by stage. You can cope, taking one step at a time, little steps and big steps, moving on along your path. Tell yourself that you can and will cope. You are ready to progress now.

Guided visualization can go much further than this, of course, but using short examples like the Chill Out exercise above will give you some idea of the effects and benefits available. If you're interested, you can always take it further.

Relaxation

Very briefly, there is one other technique which I'll mention here, which can help you relax and focus your mind when the stresses of trying to move forward are getting to you. It's a very small part of what is called autogenic training, but don't bother about the fancy title. Think of it as an extension of concentrating on your breathing, as a programme of gradually focusing on parts of your body, in order to relax both them and your mind in the process.

As it starts at your toes and works its way up to the component parts of your head, it evidently takes some time to do. If we go through one or two of the initial steps here, perhaps you can use your imagination to develop further to give yourself a better focus and inner calm. It will help you to relax – some people use it to get off to sleep at night, if the idea of counting sheep doesn't appeal!

Chill out time-18

You'll probably find it easier lying comfortably on a carpeted floor or mat for this one. If that's all too much, just sit comfortably in an easy chair. (For the purposes of the directions, I'll assume that you're lying on the floor.)

As you lie on the floor, feel your body against the surface.

Feel the points of contact and concentrate your weight on these points.

Feel any negativity from your body 'earthing' into the floor, like an electrical discharge.

Now, focus on your left foot – feel your heel against the floor.

Stretch your foot and press your weight into the heel. Flex your toes.

Feel that your left foot is very heavy – and relaxed.

Feel the extra energy from your foot draining out through your heel, into the floor.

Relax and rest for a moment.

Now, focus on your left leg calf muscles. Feel your leg heavy. Let your muscles relax.

Picture the extra energy from your lower leg drain down into your foot – and earth to the floor.

Repeat this if necessary, until your calf muscles feel relaxed.

Relax and rest for a moment.

Now, focus on your left knee cap. Flex your knee cap slightly. Feel it tensing and slackening.

End with your knee muscles relaxed. Feel the energy draining out and downwards.

Picture the flow down through your lower leg and out through your heel.

Now, relax and rest your leg for a moment.

When you're ready, focus your attention on your left thigh, and so on.

You can also try these exercises lying in a hot bath to which you have added some relaxing essential oil, such as lavender, chamomile, ylang ylang or sandalwood. Switch the light off and bathe by candlelight and you've created the perfect atmosphere for any of these exercises, to allow yourself to relax and prepare yourself for more brilliant planning in the future.

- Your mind will be more focused.
- You will be more prepared to face some of the blocks to your progress.
- You will find yourself thinking more creatively.
- You will be able to think of alternative strategies – and select the best.
- You will become more aware of how you fit into your bigger picture.

Summary

The mind is a wonderful thing, if allowed full scope. The limited success which robots and computers have had in emulating human brain capabilities gives us some idea of how vast our own potential is, to plan and respond to our brilliant future needs. We must learn to expand into this scope as fully as possible.

9 Keeping things moving forward

Now that you feel more relaxed and focused, it's time to get going on your own personal path again and view the way ahead. You can even apply your new-found visualization techniques to give it a bit more reality.

Where have we got to so far? Picture this.

- Your individual path stretches ahead, progressing down a wider track.

- This track represents the current limits of your work and life potential.

- Each path represents the progress of you as an individual.

- These paths run serpent-like, sometimes influencing each other.

- These co-operative actions may encourage faster individual progress.

- Along each path runs a series of milestones – each individual's goals.

- Many of your milestones will be the same as those of other individuals.

- Some milestones will be unique to individual development plan paths.

- Each individual, including you, progresses at his or her own rate.

- On occasion, an individual may pause to consolidate.

- On occasion, an individual may even double back slightly to try again.

- When judging progress, time is relative – sometimes fast, sometimes slow.

- You will be aware of most of the milestones which lie ahead of you.

- You may know your final goal precisely – or it may refine as you progress.

Can you visualize the overall picture now? Seeing your progress in this way may help when you come to set down your ideas in the planning system. You can picture the point at which you stand currently on the track and can foresee where the blocks may be and who you can call on for assistance. You feel confident that you can negotiate your way round these blocks, sooner or later. You can see the different subject areas you still have to tackle and will be clear on the objectives and priorities for each of these areas. By looking around, you can see the scope – or bigger picture – ahead and to the sides. You may even question at times whether the boundaries at the edge of the track need to be pushed out a bit. Not that I'm preaching revolution, of course, but if you're thinking laterally and creatively, you may find solutions which do not necessarily totally fit into existing moulds. A bit 'tall poppy' perhaps – but remember, the holistic world needs tall poppies, especially ones which can flex in the winds of change.

You should now be clear in your own mind on your sheep and goat tendencies – and how these might alter and develop as your career progresses. You will see the parallels – but you'll also be aware of the differences. You'll now have a clear idea of the actual responsibilities and tasks which each stance places on your shoulders. If you are a sheep, it's fitting more within the system. At the same time though, if you're aware of the support you can call on, you'll be learning how to make best use of these company-arranged opportunities in an open, objective way.

If you're a goat, you'll be better able to decide on the specific areas you want to develop. Remember, this direct involvement means you will be shouldering more of the responsibility for setting up the learning and development. More work, but more control over the pace and direction of your own progress. And, as either sheep or goat, you'll become clearer on the techniques and planning which you can apply to keep on moving down that development track.

We've already considered some of the key learning techniques which you can potentially use: some will suit your natural style more than others; some will be better for some subject areas than others. All can be used effectively, given the right situation. Remember some of them?

We had:

- e-learning, using computer techniques and the internet
- courses, seminars and tutorials
- open and distance learning
- coaching and mentoring
- work-based learning
- practical experience with assistance
- set programmes towards approved qualifications
- informal demonstrations and explanations
- open-ended self-study.

There may possibly be others that you can think of, or that you would also consider using – but most will be types or permutations of these.

Find out time-20

To refresh your thinking on some of the learning techniques you can use, think through the following questions.

1 If you have your own internet link, what are some of the key benefits of e-learning?

2 Which of your planned learning areas would be helped by having human support?

3 Think of two or three specific areas and identify exactly what support would be useful.

---

4 With 'interactive learning', which types of interactivity would you find useful?

---

5 What would you see as the benefits of 'work-based learning', practising on-the-job?

---

6 What are the benefits and disadvantages of just 'figuring things out for myself'?

---

7 Is gaining a qualification important to you? If so, which one(s) would you like to achieve?

---

8 Can you learn from reading books or do you need to complete written exercises as well?

---

9 How do you find out details of the range of learning resources which are available?

---

10 What features of coaching and mentoring attract you?

You may remember that we covered a lot of this earlier. If you feel you need to, check back on Chapter 6. We haven't yet focused on coaching and mentoring, so here are a few thoughts on this to help you expand on question 10.

Mentoring and coaching

I have already mentioned in Chapter 6 what I call 'the integrated triangle', with the model linking the individual with support from the training and development department and assistance from mentors.

It looks like this.

We'll come back to it in greater detail in Chapter 12. I use the simple term 'mentors' for ease of reference but there are elements of coaching in the role as well.

Individual

Mentor

Development support

Traditionally, a mentor is a revered figure (like Plato, for instance) who takes an individual or individuals under his or her wing and 'grows' each individual, often involving a one-to-one relationship over a period of time. Some companies use mentoring to 'fast-track' an individual to prepare him or her for being a senior manager or director or whatever. In short, the traditional definition gives a mentoring relationship between two people, which goes on over a period of time as the one imparts wisdom and knowledge to the other.

Coaching is taking someone who already has some skill and/or knowledge and helping them focus on that level of skill and working with them to develop the skill further, to a higher level. Some think that it's not necessary for the coach to be expert in the skill being coached – perhaps the jury's still out on that one. But the important point is that the individual is being helped to analyse, develop and progress a pre-existing skill. The coach, if you like, is acting as a catalyst, to help the individual's natural skill develop.

This is where the holistic thinking bit comes into play. Think of your colleagues and friends for a minute. Think of the number of skills and vast range of specialist knowledge that they have. Think of the experience and wisdom that they could pass on to others. OK, some have more than others – and we have to consider the need to shift attitudes towards acting as mentors and coaching with some people – but focus on all that potential for a moment. Now, think of the skills and knowledge and experience and wisdom which you have, that you could pass on to someone else. (Of course you have – just think about it for a minute or two!)

Take any company. If you're in a sheep situation, think of the staff in your company. Think of all the expertise represented in there, that could be passed on to other company personnel who lack it. I accept it's not an easy option – there's the time element, which we'll come back to – and the attitudinal thing of people not seeing why they should be involved. It helps if people can see this transfer of knowledge as two-way.

I'm good at writing reports but have never used Excel. You use Excel on a daily basis; the departmental manager has a problem with setting out his reports formally. I help him sort out his report writing problems; you help me come to grips with Excel. You, in turn, have some learning need which can be helped by someone else. Everyone can get involved, if the atmosphere's right. Think of it as a complete learning circle, as the intense activity makes the integrated triangle revolve. We all benefit – even the act of being a mentor is part of development. It gives us experience in a range of skills, including dealing with people, logical thought, delivery technique, knowledge and skills analysis, open questioning and technology transfer.

360° mentoring can make the world go round – faster and better!

It becomes slightly harder to find your sources if you're more in a goat situation – but it is possible through networking and other opportunities of getting together. This chain-reaction sharing of skills and knowledge, or '360° mentoring', is the real benefit or outcome of the whole process, with people genuinely helping each other. That's how the mentoring part of the integrated triangle works – altruistically.

OK, there are certainly elements of coaching in there as well and the traditional old/young, senior/junior roles of mentoring are not considered necessary. Accept that but just go with the simple title 'mentoring', for ease of reference. The important thing is getting as many people as possible involved in helping each other. Status and qualifications are secondary; enthusiasm and positive attitude are key. Qualified coaches might take offence at everyone calling themselves coaches but as far as I know there are no mentoring qualifications, so the brief is more open-ended. Potentially, under the definition I use, you are a mentor, I am a mentor – virtually everyone can be a mentor, given a bit of help along the way to think objectively, apply help and understanding and plan brilliantly. This is what you are doing as an individual. So, where the system is in place for the integrated triangle to operate:

- you, as the *individual*, can look for help from
- a range of *mentors* and call on support and resources
- from *training and development support*.

While at other times, you will be the mentor, helping another individual.

Thus, you'll be an individual on some ocasions; a mentor on others. If you happen to work in the Training and Development Department, you're potentially involved in all three corners of the triangle and could be any one of the three at any given learning moment.

It's a simple process, if the attitudes are right and the support's in place. But it's a very valuable process, greatly expanding the potential for personal and professional development and lifelong learning activities. Once you've thought about the potential and warm to the idea, do your bit by suggesting that it happens in your area of learning. It provides a vast potential resource for the Training and Development Department to use – but it does need a lot of background organization, of a different kind to that which they may be used to providing. Initially crossing the fence can be a bit hard.

One of the problems with encouraging people to get involved in mentoring is the time factor. Responses can include, 'It's the trainers' job. Let them organize their courses and our departments will release the staff to attend'.

What isn't necessarily recognized is that a course means members of staff being away for days at a time and often being exposed to more information than they can hope to retain. As the training's often general, to suit different needs, some of it's not relevant. Perhaps if the learning was carried out in smaller chunks, in the actual workplace – and perhaps, if the trainers or whoever is guiding the learning knew the real priorities of the department, the learning could be applied more directly.

It would certainly need some input first of all, to help people's attitudes, sort out the ground rules of how the mentoring process works and give some simple ideas of how to structure the learning and get the message across well. You could certainly make the training very relevant, deliver it in bite-sized chunks and make sure that it was reinforced properly afterwards. Knowing more about what was going on, you could check that standards were being met.

And it's a two-way process: perhaps you spend some more of your time being involved in mentoring others, but then they'll work smarter – so that'll save time in the department, if you're a sheep person. As a learner, you'll benefit from being mentored by others in the office or workplace, so that will save time as well. And the whole mentoring process will mean that those involved will work more closely as a team, which will make you all more efficient.

Managing your time to achieve your objectives

So, we have the techniques for achieving the learning. We also need to spend some time considering other methods which, if applied well, will help our planned activities happen. When we've been charting our progress along the development path and when we've been reviewing the priorities for planning our own brilliant futures, we're always conscious of the time element. Sometimes, things take a long time to con-solidate. Sometimes, if our plans are ahead of their time as far as general needs are concerned, we may have to wait, accepting that progress will have to go 'on ice' for a while. And sometimes, by managing our time as effectively as possible, we can move things along smartly, achieving our goals and objectives as rapidly as possible.

Find out time-21

Let's find out some of the key issues which take up too much of your time. Make notes.

1   How could your own personal control of your time be simplified?

2   What activity would you highlight, which wastes the greatest amount of your time each day?

3   At which period(s) of the day do you usually work most efficiently?

4   How do you monitor your progress towards achieving goals and mile-stones?

5   In which ways can a planning system help you make best use of your time?

6 How can you control the way others influence your daily plans?

_____

7 How can you use long- and short-term goals to make best use of your time?

Individual development planning and personal time planning knit very closely together – they have to, because they both involve you directly. How often have you heard someone say, 'I really need to do that … if only I had time'?

And how often is the 'that' which needs doing, linked in some way with the individual's development? We've already spoken about prioritizing our development needs in terms of the activities which need to be sorted out soon and those which are longer term. Just to complicate matters some more, think of your development needs as one pile adding to the total mound you need to do on a daily basis:

- letters and e-mails to write
- widgets to produce
- people to speak to
- reports to plan and write
- phone calls to make
- preparations to complete; _and_
- development needs to progress.

Prioritization is an art and the more flexible you can be, the better.

Prioritization

Think of three category levels: A, B and C.

Category A includes things which are part of your direct day-to-day responsibilities, which need to be completed by the end of each working day. In the competency-driven world in which we now find ourselves, think of category 'A' tasks as the ones you will be measured on. They need to be watched closely to make sure you're progressing OK with them – and they usually have deadlines which must be met.

Category B tasks are still part of the direct responsibilities in your work – but can be judged as being less important at any given time. As with everything, priorities will shift, so it is largely the 'B' tasks which give this flexibility. Something which is a 'B' category today may well become an 'A' category tomorrow (because, for example, the deadline is getting closer). Sometimes, you can do bits of 'B' category tasks but leave them incomplete, if you've forward planned and are giving yourself enough time. This fits in neatly with planning where you come up against blocks – allowing you to juggle with several developmental balls in the air at the same time.

Category C are activities which are not important and are not your direct responsibility. For this reason, you won't be judged on whether you complete them – so they're things which have a low priority. So, delegate them, or postpone them until you've got some spare time. Often, they're 'comfort tasks', easy to do, like photocopying or fetching the coffees, for example, but not really what you are being paid to do.

There is a style of management called 'managing by walking about' or MBWA. The original thinking behind this was that some managers never got out of their offices so had little idea what was going on within their department or unit. By actually experiencing the work being carried out and speaking to their staff, they could see some of the problems and frustrations at first hand and then do something about it. That would be a 'B' activity level, with periodic 'A' outcomes.

Some managers are happiest 'getting their hands dirty' and spending large chunks of time on the shop floor. Meanwhile, the real work they're actually being paid to do – the policy decisions, reports, forward planning, staffing matters and all the other management responsibilities – pile up on the desk back in the office. That's not good MBWA – that's just escapism.

There's also a fourth category, or rather it's a rider that can attach to any one of the others.

Category X is used to change the priority rating in an emergency or crisis, or where there is a high-priority demand. 'High-priority demands' are a bit suspect. They're OK where there is a genuine emergency but if they've merely come about because the boss is disorganized and has forgotten about the key report summary or whatever which he needs for a meeting tomorrow, that's not good. But then, if you're in a position to delegate, you never resort to that, do you? Do you?

Using this judgement system, a 'BX' activity could take priority over an 'A' activity. You could, for example, be working on your report for tomorrow when Harry asks for the key points of a speech which you are to give in three days. At this point, certainly a lower priority, planning-wise – until it is explained that this is so that Harry can produce the animated PowerPoint visuals programme for you, which will take a day or so to complete. So, that becomes justifiable.

It raises another point, though. Let's say your day is already filled with nothing but 'A' category tasks. If you drop everything to sort out this 'BX' activity, some of the 'A' activities will suffer, or you'll have to work late – again. So, your planning becomes a very flexible thing, a bit like one of these puzzles where you slide squares around within a frame, to make a picture. Think of each of the squares as an activity, with a starting off priority. Moving things around, you alter the priority as you complete different tasks – finally finishing with the completed picture again. Most people's 'things to do' lists usually incorporate a mixture of different levels of tasks, however, so the scope for flexibility is usually there.

Prioritization like this works on a day-to-day basis, for diary planning; it works in the 'bigger picture' as well, for your development planning. The two intermingle where you can be working on part of your longer-term development as an 'A'-level task – but you may well consider it as a 'B' task in your daily 'things to do' list. The world will not collapse if you put it off until tomorrow. And so planning continues.

Cross-relationships

That's quite a clear illustration of the cross-relationship between short- and long-term planning. There are several other relationships we should consider, when we're looking at planning from the broader perspective.

Work out time-22

1   What's the relationship between a task and a goal?

Think goal – think milestone.

The task, on the other hand, is what you do in order to achieve the goal.

2   What's the difference between reactive and proactive?

Given the clue that they're opposites, you react to something that's already happened.

Proactive thinking is very valuable for forward planning – it helps you work your way round some of the blockages too. My earlier points regarding lateral thinking illustrate this.

3   How about the relationship between routine and innovative tasks?

We all have our routines, whether it's getting up, travelling to work or the 'daily grind'.

Lots of people will look out for innovative tasks to complete, to break the monotony of the day. For others, however, innovation makes their brains hurt! There may well be a bit of creative, or lateral thinking involved. The ground rules will certainly be more open-ended.

4   And finally, what's the relationship between activity and outcome?

The outcome's the more important bit here. You can attend a seminar or you can spend the afternoon working, doing some practical exercise or other. Both of these are activities, but what are the outcomes (or outputs, if you prefer)? We can only check whether an activity has been worth the effort and we've really achieved something if we're clear what the outcome or objective is – and can use it to measure our success.

Summary

So, managing our time carefully helps us plan better and helps us head towards that brilliant future. Overall, better control of our destiny means more confidence, less stress and more possibility of that whoopee factor getting us out of bed in the morning with a feeling of excitement.

Managing our time; managing our development – managing ourselves.

Let's round off this chapter with some food for thought, summarizing some of the considerations we've been kicking around. Relax and think about them a bit.

Chill out time-19

How can you manage your time better, giving yourself more time for the interesting things in life? Find yourself a quiet spot and focus on each of the following for a moment or two:

- learn to say 'No' nicely
- keep a flexible view of your own priorities
- concentrate first on your 'A' priorities
- explain your stance where required
- plan ahead
- if you accept extra work, something's got to flex
- stand back regularly and see the bigger picture

- write things down – it helps you visualize
- update your 'things to do' list regularly
- think in actions
- focus on your planned outcomes
- use your peak working times to best advantage
- use minimum time to maximum effect
- give yourself 'time outs' or thinking time
- pinpoint sources of stress – and face up to them
- be aware of your responsibilities
- if delegating, brief properly, then let them get on with it
- empowerment needs encouragement in order to succeed
- help is a two-way process – offer as well as receive.

There's a lot in there to think about to make best use of your time – and allow some of it to plan your brilliant future. Longer-term plans have perhaps tended towards being the ones that gradually get pushed further and further back because we never get round to doing them – until they hit the panic fan.

Getting a proper planning system in place will make sure that your work and life plans progress as you want them to.

It's time to study the *ID Plan* personal planning system in greater detail.

part four

for
go
it

And finally … coming to grips with the *ID Plan* system. Details of the format pages and how to complete them; ways of finding your acceptable work/life balance and some final thoughts and tips before you set off along your chosen development path.

10 Planning for that brilliant future

Let's get some of the ground rules sorted out first.

ID Plan is a flexible personal planning system, with the 'I D' standing for Individual Development. It also involves your personal 'identity' as well, linking your inner being seamlessly with its outer organization. As it's flexible, it can be used for both sheep and goat scenarios, by selecting the format pages from the system which *you* find both appropriate and useful.

And this is the important bit. No-one's saying you have to plough your way through each of the format pages, filling in copious amounts of information. That's a big turn-off. What I am saying is: here's a series of pages of questions, check points and response boxes to use in a way that you find valuable, so that you can get a better handle on your own future progress.

You may use different sequences and permutations for different elements of your future plans. That's fine. If it's valuable to you, you'll see the benefits of using *ID Plan* to some degree and the whole process will work for you. Many of the format page fields are fairly self-explanatory; some need to be spelled out a bit so that you can see how to use them to meet a variety of needs. What we'll do is go through each one in turn, explaining as necessary. Scan through this detail to get a general idea. You'll probably find that it's only when you come to use the system for real that you have to go back to study specific points about how to use the format pages.

You've already been introduced to the system and the thinking behind it in the second half of Chapter 7. You can access it from the website, on *www.business-minds.com* and there are also reduced copies of the format pages in the Appendix at the end of this book.

You can print off copies of the system from the website for your own use and respond to the questions by hand-completing the boxes in writing or typing. The formats are also designed so that you can enter data directly into the fields on-screen, then print off each completed format page.

Format 12 is designed for sheep internal company use, to register completed outcomes for your Continuing Professional Development (CPD) records. (Apologies in advance for the flurry of jargon in this particular format page. It's designed so that you can use it directly as a record document for your Training and HR Department, if they keep these kinds of records. It's using the usual 'CPD speak' (which I explain later in this chapter) – so you'll know what they're talking about and appear knowledgeable in the discussions!)

There is another format (Format 15) which is designed in an open-ended way, with open entry fields, so that you can create your own 'bridge' pages. Use this to satisfy your own needs if you feel there's a gap in the overall *ID Plan* system, as far as your future planning is concerned.

So that's where to find it and how it works, overall. The next stage is to go through each format and explain the thinking behind it – and how to complete it. As I've already said, don't get bogged down in the detail at this stage – just scan through to get the general feel for the formats and how they link together.

We'll start off by reviewing the sequence of format pages and their basic uses.

ID Plan Format Pages

Format 1. Strengths and Shortfalls

An opportunity to focus on what you're good at and identify the areas which you need to develop further (or find an alternative strategy).

Format 2. Specific Development Areas

A personal brainstorm of what you see as your main areas for future development, with first thoughts about ways of achieving them – and their priority order.

Format 3. Development Routes – Sheep Employee Aspect

A sequence of responses to trigger ideas of help and support which you can call on from your employer, to achieve your development goals.

Format 4. Development Routes – Goat Independent Aspect

A parallel sequence of responses to trigger ideas of help and support which you can source from networking and other external sources, to achieve your development goals.

Format 5. Am I going in the right direction?

A pause for thought, to check that your development plans are in fact leading you in a direction that you really want to take, certainly in the foreseeable future.

Formats 6–12

These are completed in relation to each Development Area identified.

This means that your folder will gradually build up sets of these format sequences, filed under each Development Area heading, as you achieve each outcome.

Format 6. Overall Plan for a specified Development Area

A first response to writing the objective statement, deciding on possible techniques and steps and stages to be applied – and other details of how you would like your learning programme to take place.

Format 7. Development Action Plan

Key questions to which you can respond, to get you thinking in detail about how your learning programme for this development area can get going and progress.

Format 8. Theory in Practice – Sheep Employee Aspect

A sequence of questions to put your planned learning activities within the context of your job, to highlight any potential blocks and ways of reinforcing the learning.

Format 9. Theory in Practice – Goat Independent Aspect

A sequence of questions to relate your planned learning activities to your self-employed status, to highlight possible blocks and ways of reinforcing the learning.

Format 10. Identifying the Support

Drawing together and expanding on earlier information, to capture ideas for making this development area happen, in specific terms of people, resources and funding.

Format 11. Checking on Progress – Informal

A series of check questions to ask, to establish that the planned progress is happening on time and following the expected sequence and milestones.

Format 12. Checking on Progress – Formal (Optional)

This is the CPD Record Form referred to at the start of this chapter, which logs the information which may be requested by the Training/HR Department for your records.

Formats 13–15

These relate to you generally and not to a specific Development Area.

Format 13. Personal Development prompts

Questions to help you consider yourself more holistically – to consider how you can lead a fuller life and become more involved in 'Bigger Picture' thinking.

Format 14. Action Plan – Present and Future

A general sheet for noting down long-term plans and more immediate 'things to do', in order to keep an overview of your progress and required activities.

Format 15. Open completion

An open format to use if you need any additional prompts which are not included in the *ID Plan* planning system as presented. Both heading and data completion fields are active, for creation on-screen.

Using the *ID Plan* system

These are the 15 formats which follow a logical sequence gradually delving more deeply into the needs for developing each of your identified areas. This sequence also provides periodic stages to confirm and recap on progress. Looking at your development in a broader way, some of the elements which are included will encourage you to see the bigger picture. This is necessary if you want your work/life balance to be more co-operative and stress-free.

However, my logic may not be yours, so tailor the system to suit your own logic and priorities.

As you've been progressing through the book so far, and responding to the various exercise sections, you've been gradually refining your own thinking about planning your brilliant future. You've been developing the ideas necessary to apply in selecting the most appropriate path from the *ID Plan* system format pages and their content. You might find it useful at this stage to review the responses you may have made.

Work out time-23

Here are the main exercises you have done which link in directly with developing your planning system priorities. Check back for any responses you made, or have a look at the exercises again and think through your responses, now that you are clearer on the structure.

- FIND OUT Time 6, page 40
- FIND OUT Time 7, page 41
- FIND OUT Time 8, page 43
- WORK OUT Time 7, page 45
- CHILL OUT Time 6, page 47
- FIND OUT Time 10, page 53
- WORK OUT Time 9, page 56
- CHILL OUT Time 8, page 58
- FIND OUT Time 11, page 60
- WORK OUT Time 11, page 65
- FIND OUT Time 13, page 77
- CHILL OUT Time 10, page 83
- CHILL OUT Time 11, page 88
- FIND OUT Time 15, page 97
- FIND OUT Time 17, page 108
- WORK OUT Time 19, page 112
- FIND OUT Time 18, page 115
- CHILL OUT Time 15, page 117
- WORK OUT Time 21, page 127
- FIND OUT Time 20, page 141
- WORK OUT Time 22, page 151

These exercises and responses have been helping you to focus and clarify your own needs and priorities when it comes to developing and using an individual development planning system such as *ID Plan*. If you study them – and the ways you responded – you will get an idea of how closely your own plans link with those of the sequence in the planning system. Check out *WORK OUT Time 19* again, as it's special. In it, we worked through a sequence of planning steps and stages which will be mirrored by the way we use the range of formats provided in the *ID Plan* system. It's worth checking once more how our logic flowed.

Now, it's time to consider each format in greater detail, to make sure that there's no confusion in completing the detail. Don't worry about this detail too much though; if there's any particular question or response that you don't understand, or can't see its relevance, just miss it out.

This is empowerment – so you're working on planning and developing your own brilliant future. But you're not alone, remember. There are lots of people around to help – to give advice, help and clarification. Think about seeking second opinions sometimes as well, especially if you're thinking of a fairly major change in direction. Getting a range of opinions should help you reach more objective decisions – hard to take, on occasion, but often worth their weight in the long term.

ID Plan – Operational Notes

The 15 formats of the *ID Plan* system follow, together with explanations of how best to use them. The applications will vary with particular development areas; they will also vary with particular individuals. It's a flexible system – use it as best suits your own needs.

Format 1 (Appendix, page 215)

This is an exercise you did in the early stages of the book.

With some strengths, you've perhaps reached your peak – unless you really want to specialize. With others, you will be able to identify the development path you should progress along.

Question 3 is asking for your immediate ideas about ways you would like to learn and develop and reinforce that learning. Nothing in-depth here but go on your first thoughts. Do you need to attend a course, or would you prefer to study at home through e-learning programmes? Can you pick up enough from reading a book on the subject – or would you develop best through coaching and mentoring on the job? You may find this quite hard to do initially but once you've had experience of a range of different techniques, selecting the best options should get easier.

Question 4 looks at what to do about shortfalls which you would find very difficult to improve upon. Initially, you might have to think very carefully whether it's worth the effort involved, to end up gaining a very small improvement. The same amount of effort might improve another shortfall or strength quite a lot. If you're thought of as being very competent – an expert, even – in some skills, you can afford to leave others to one side. In these cases, you can compensate either by delegating or by finding ways round the blockages.

Alternatively, once you've identified the shortfall in real terms, you can then focus on ways of improving it. It could just be lack of knowledge or practical experience. Sometimes, the greatest motivator for really getting down to developing or improving a new skill is knowing that you're going to be responsible for doing it. Today, you're work-shadowing; tomorrow, you'll be on your own. Initial panic but focused learning. If this is the way ahead, establish priorities and get the practice.

Format 2 (Appendix, page 216)

This page captures your ideas of which development areas are important to you. Have a mini brainstorm to yourself and write down up to six areas which you feel you need to work on further. Don't worry about the priority – just get the information down. You can put in the priority rating later (1–6 in order).

Under the 'Initial Action Notes' for each, record any development ideas you have. It might be people you have to talk to, books you might read or methods you could use to extract the information. Practical experience is usually a very important element of overall development, so you can also note ideas of how to get this practice here.

Once you have completed this page, you should have:

- sorted out your development areas
- established the priority
- noted ideas of how you would prefer to progress
- listed some particular learning ideas.

Format 3 (Appendix, page 217)

This (sheep) page is for you if you work within some form of company or organization, where you can expect backup and support.

Questions 1 and 2 are an opportunity to record any of the sources of help that you've come across. It might be individuals with expertise they are happy passing on – or situations where you can get some practical help. Remember, practice is all-important in any new learning, so search out effective ways of getting this.

Question 3 is recognizing that your priorities may be different from those of the organization – so you might find it difficult drumming up enthusiasm for some of your personal development ideas. If you're really keen on doing something, keep it on active hold in your mind and use oportunities when they present themselves – which they will, ultimately.

Questions 4 and 5 are considering informal and formal ways of gaining further development. Sometimes, the formal ways might be approached in a fairly mechanical, prescriptive way. Use this structure to your advantage but try to inject a bit of imagination into it.

Question 6 is for recording any contact names mentioned during your discussions. They are like gold dust and can save you immense amounts of time later. Often, they act as a chain reaction – person A may not be able to help on this occasion – but gives you person B's details, and so on. File them for future reference as well but remember that assistance should be two-way. Offer as well as receive help.

Format 4 (Appendix, page 218)

This is the goat equivalent of Format 3, for the self-employed and others 'outside the sheep system'. The questions are thus seeking answers to similar or parallel situations.

Questions 1 and 2 are trying to identify contact names – both individual and providers. Networking is very important for the individual who doesn't have a company structure to fall back upon – try to make best use of the process.

Question 3 is encouraging you to establish your different milestones – both short and longer term – to help you see the steps and stages of the way ahead. You're focusing on your priorities here but seeing them in the long term as well as the short. Note also any ideas of how you might best progress them.

Question 4 is a bit of a brainstorm on some of the things which could stand in your way. Some of these you obviously won't know about at this stage – but you may be aware of problems other people have had.

Question 5 is getting into specific detail. There's no particular reason why you should know about this kind of information but it's always amazing the way, when you start talking to other people, you pick up on ideas, books to read, resources to check out, useful telephone numbers, other people to contact and so on. Make a note of them, as some at least will be worth following up.

Question 6 is encouraging you to think of your own preferences. You will be happier learning in some ways than others. You would enjoy some types of practice more than others. There might be some areas of practical experience that you've always fancied trying. This is your chance to choose things that really motivate you. Have fun!

Format 5 (Appendix, page 219)

This is an opportunity to do a double take on your thoughts so far. If your future planning is actually moving you in a different direction, here's a chance to check whether you're sure it's right for you. The questions are not there to discourage you – just to give you a chance to review, confirm or perhaps refine your thoughts.

Questions 1 and 2 will encourage you to be as specific as possible – and when you've set down your ideas, stand back and debate with yourself, to make sure you feel positive about progressing further towards the goal you've set yourself.

One of the best ways to sort out the theory and dreams from the reality is to talk to someone who is actually doing the thing you dream of doing. Or try to experience it at first hand. **Question 3** prompts you to do this. Think about what you want to ask them before you speak to them, and really listen to the answers – don't ignore what you don't want to hear. Note down any hints and tips as well – it's never too early to be prepared.

A double check to make sure you really want to go in the direction you're heading. **Question 4** helps you there. A keen fly fisherman doesn't necessarily make a good fishing tackle shop owner; a successful salesperson doesn't necessarily make an efficient sales manager. Or, if you're thinking of giving up your job and writing for a living, for example, does it have to be as a 'best selling author'? There are other writing options open. Encouragement to step out and back from yourself for a moment – have an 'out of body experience' and check that you're really suited for the plans you have for yourself.

There are lots of psychometric and similar tests available now to check on your competencies, priorities and preferences. There are books of them – try the Internet, ask HR. **Question 5** gives you the chance to log any details of sources for these tests. If you feel they're valuable and will be comfortable working with the results, try some of these tests. See what they come up with regarding your future career path.

Question 6 – these milestones again. If you can look down your track and see the goal milestone in the distance, you should be able to establish the smaller stones mapping out the way ahead. If you're maybe being too ambitious with your main goal, this will help you revise things slightly – but still be on the right track.

Question 7 speaks for itself. You don't need to have doubts – don't scratch your head trying to think of some. But if you do have any – get them down on paper and try to think of answers. By the end of this format, you should be more confident that you're making the right decisions, or else you may have to go back and revise some of your earlier thoughts.

Format 6 (Appendix, page 220)

This is the first of a series of formats, the *ID Plan* format pages 6–12, which focus on one Development Area and follow it through the steps and stages of progress. If you look again at Format 2 on page 216, this registered up to six different areas and got you to sort out a priority sequence. Format 6 then becomes the first detailed format logging details, of your highest priority area, which you will then plan through more and more deeply as you progress to Formats 11 and 12, the final stages of achieving your goal, or meeting your objective.

Think of writing objectives when you're completing **Question 1**. Set it down as an action statement and think what it is you're trying to achieve. It's that end goal we were speaking about in the previous format. It's all about objective thinking – remember the widgets – check out Chapter 5 again if you need to.

Question 2. Think about what it is you hope to achieve. Is it something physical you have to do? Is it mainly knowledge? Does it involve dealing directly with people? Does it use computer skills? What styles of learning do you generally prefer? Think objectively and you'll realize that some techniques will be better than others for helping you learn any particular subject effectively. For factual knowledge and step-by-step processes – use e-learning; for dealing with people directly – use role plays or workplace learning. Common sense, if you think about it.

We've already thought about some of the intermediate milestones. **Question 3** is a chance to think more and more deeply about this specific development area and get your thoughts down on paper in an orderly fashion. Remember – think *actions*.

Questions 4 and 5, once again, are firming up on specifics for this particular development area. As you become clearer on the information you will cover and the activities you will need to do to reinforce the learning, you can note these ideas down.

If you've written the statements as actions, you should be pretty close to having 'outcomes' already, to satisfy **Question 6**. If you need to, check in Chapter 5 again. When you're setting off to write each statement, start the sentence by thinking: *On reaching this particular milestone, I will be capable of ...* This will help you focus on what it is you want to do, so that you'll be able to check when you've achieved it – and reached your outcome.

Question 7 is encouraging you to think 'bigger picture'. Don't just sit with your nose close to this particular development area. Look around and see how it links in with others. See how experience in another area might help reinforce this one. Where are the connections? Maybe they affect the way you'll progress with this area. Maybe your abilities in other areas will improve your achievement holistically in this one.

Format 7 (Appendix, page 221)

This is an action plan for progressing with this development area. You've looked at the scenario from various different angles; figured out the priorities; recorded the people you can speak to and the resources and techniques you can use – all in general terms.

Format 7 is getting down to specifics. The questions are straightforward. Some relate to previous, more general detail you've sorted through. They don't need any further explanation. Do be specific.

Format 8 (Appendix, page 222)

Formats 8 and 9 are subdivisions for sheep and goat situations again. You won't need to do both – one will be more relevant than the other to your particular situation.

Format 8 is basically helping you check how your ideas and priorities fit in with the business ones where you work. We've talked about this earlier – things are more likely to happen for you where your needs fit those of the business. You want to improve your communication skills – your boss has plans for making you a team leader and wants you to run daily meetings, for example. Mutually beneficial so there shouldn't be much problem reaching agreement. Don't feel that you have to compromise too much though – remember the flexing tall poppy. It just takes longer. The questions in Format 8 will help you plan your own strategies.

Questions 1–3 are helping you come to terms with how your personal priorities stand against those of the business. Face up to the comparisons – don't pretend they're not there, or don't matter. Use your selling and negotiating skills. Think of benefits for the company which will result from the things that you want to do. Unless your plans are totally egocentric or off the wall, there's usually some joint benefits there, if you search around. You may have to flex on priority and timing a bit though. Good things are worth waiting for. If you believe in something, there will be a way of making it happen – ultimately.

In **Question 4**, 'levels of support' can be taken from different angles. It could be from individuals: your boss, or the training manager, for example. It could be financial; it could be in terms of facilities available. Think of the support you require for this particular development area and the type and extent of the help and support you reckon is necessary. Any ideas you have for influencing it further go down as responses to **Question 5**.

Questions 6 and 7 are encouraging you to think 'bigger picture' again. Not in terms of other areas this time but more looking into the future. Statistics show that it's often easier to move internally within a company and get involved in doing something new than trying on the open market where lack of relevant experience will be a disadvantage. Keep your ear to the ground, read the company magazine and use any other legal means of keeping informed about the company's plans. Then you can perhaps do something to get a bit of relevant experience or be in the right position when the new ideas become public and they're looking for specialist staff. It need not be long term. It might give you that bit of experience which makes you more marketable – to help you set off in your alternative direction, if that's what your long-term plan involves.

Question 8 is refining the milestones again. Nothing new in doing it – just a chance to review and revise, progressively becoming more and more precise.

Question 9 is a more precise form of Question 1, written in 'business speak'. No apologies for this – it's to encourage you to think that way before you go and discuss your needs with officialdom. It helps to be able to speak their language when you're fighting your corner, otherwise you appear vague. Use words like 'criteria', 'facilitate', 'benchmark' and 'objective' and you'll have them eating out of your hand (as long as you check out what they mean beforehand!)

Format 9 (Appendix, page 223)

This follows a parallel path to Format 8 but, because it is designed with the goat situation in mind, it relies more on the individual doing things him or herself. So, there's less about trying to fit in with company plans and bosses and more about networking and finding help informally, as well as formally, where possible.

If you've been thinking in action terms, **Questions 1 and 2** should be fairly straightforward. You should be clear about what you're trying to do by this stage, so this detail will help you get going, especially as you have more control over your destiny being a goat person. The budget may be limited but the opportunities are not.

Getting the additional experience can be a bit harder, if it involves facilities or contacts which you don't have full access to at the moment. This is where networking helps. If it involves a new piece of kit, which you are in a position to buy, you can perhaps get this and give yourself the experience, with a bit of help from your friends and contacts. Buy it from a company where you can demand a bit of direct training, rather than saving a few pounds by getting it by impersonal e-mail order, or similar, where they are often more concerned with box shifting than user support.

Question 3 needs a bit of thought. It's suggesting that, if you think closely about what it is you want to do and how you can apply it, you can tighten up the expected actions in your goals and objectives. If they're precise and written with your facilities and capabilities in mind, there's more chance of getting the required experience. As I hope I convinced you earlier in Chapter 5, it's worth worrying away at the wording and content of objectives, as it ultimately makes reaching the goals much easier.

Question 4 is another logging point for networking details. There's an amazing amount of support around if you go out looking for it. Your friendly local enterprise/learning & skills council will have various seminars and programmes on offer and there are usually business or professional associations in your area, if you seek them out. There are perhaps opportunities to swap mentoring and coaching assistance with others in a similar position – harder to organize but certainly possible. Your local colleges will have courses and programmes you can tap into, again Learndirect (or Learndirect Scotland) is a good reference source see page 93 for details of how to contact them.

We've considered the bigger picture earlier, as far as companies are concerned. **Question 5** is encouraging you to look along your development path and see how it all ties in with your own future plans and how it links in with the potential of the overall track of options. If you have a grand master plan, you will sometimes be seeking half-way experience which will act as a stepping stone – or milestone – towards achieving your ultimate goal. A number of people in radio and TV broadcasting started off as volunteers in the local hospital or community radio station, for example. There are ICT consultants who used their time as an employee within an organization to experience a range of packages or attend accreditation courses. This is your chance to slot the outcomes of this particular development area into your future overall hopes and plans. It always helps to see the bigger picture.

Question 6 is another of those review opportunities. Now that you have thought things through in greater detail, are there any slight changes you could make which would make your progress easier? Perhaps refining the area you want to develop, changing the sequence, altering the priorities, refocusing on the key people you want to involve. It all helps makes the overall plan work better – and smarter.

As with Question 8 in the previous format, **Question 7** here is an opportunity to review and tighten up on those milestones.

Question 8 in this Format gives you the chance, while thinking about the specifics of working on your development, to note down any ideas you have for the best ways of doing it. You don't have to go into vast detail, but there will probably be ways that you see as being most appropriate for these particular goals – courses rather than self-study; short modules rather than being away for days – anything that comes to mind as being worth considering when you come to firming up your plans.

Format 10 (Appendix, page 224)

This format provides a summary and a chance to bring together your thinking so far. As a recap, it's going over things you have already set down elsewhere so there could be a feeling of duplication, especially for the straightforward development areas. If it helps to refine your thinking – use it all or use parts of it. It's certainly useful for those slightly more complex or detailed development areas, where the specifics can get lost in the detail. With these, regular reviews are crucial to keeping the view ahead as clear as possible.

However, if you feel you've already clarified many of these points in your mind, feel free to skip over some or all of this format page and move on. The choice, as always, is yours.

Questions 1–4 are pretty straightforward.

Question 5 is looking towards what I call 'bridges'. When you look at the range of commercial learning opportunities around, you'll probably find that it meets some large percentage of your needs. There may be gaps, however. Perhaps the material is too general and doesn't address the specifics of your type of business; perhaps some of the exercises or case studies are not really relevant; perhaps there are just gaps in the coverage of the learning areas you want to study. This is where you will need extra input to bridge the gaps – so we have 'bridges' or 'bridge materials'. At this stage, you're more concerned with spotting the gaps than bothering too much about how to build the bridge. That comes later.

Question 6 is a chance to record the results of your networking and/or discussions regarding support and help. I stress the use of the word 'informal' here. It's not always necessary to go on a course to learn about something. Talking to the guy who actually does it is sometimes much more enlightening. Spread your net wide to catch as much as possible for this question – and don't throw the smaller fish away.

Question 7 is bringing you towards reaching a conclusion. You can go on researching and discussing, always hoping for that big break just round the corner, but ultimately, you have to go with what's available and best, given all the circumstances. This is where the bridges come in, to fill the gaps. But, ultimately, decide and commit – and get going. There's always the scope for flexibility as you progress – remember the meandering paths along the track. But it's important that the blob of energy at the head of the path – you – keeps progressing forward overall.

The final question – who pays? – is an important one. More so for goats than sheep. Within companies, there will often be budgets that can be spent, but where expenditure has to be justified. That underlines the value of previous consideration as to how well your objectives help achieve the business objectives.

When you're on your own, cost matters. There are sources of finance available though – learning accounts, subsidized seminars and resource lending libraries, for example, as well as various start-up grants and support, if you ask around.

Format 11 (Appendix, page 225)

This format is giving you a structure upon which to base your evaluation – both as an ongoing check of progress and a final confirmation of achieved objectives/outcomes.

There's a lot of talk about evaluation but not enough real action. You get 'happy sheets' at the end of courses and measurements against improved productivity and so on. We want to have measurements which can check progress and alter the path at that point, if it's not going in the correct direction. This is where precisely written objectives can help.

Imagine you're on holiday abroad. It's your main holiday of the year and something's not right, two days into your ten-day holiday. You want it sorted now, so that the rest of the holiday is OK again. It's no great comfort putting up with the problem for the remainder of the holiday, then complaining afterwards. It's the same if you're on a training course which is not meeting its stated objectives. Try to get it sorted out now – don't wait to complain at the end. These checks on progress will highlight any fine-tuning that needs to be done. Evaluation should be an ongoing process. So, Format 11 is important.

Question 1 – those milestones again. It's the small or sub-objectives which build towards reaching your final objective. Giving you your stated outcomes. If you're not reaching your milestones, is it a time thing or have the milestones shifted? Worth checking out, as the responses will be different.

The answer to the first part of **Question 2** should be 'Yes'. There's almost always scope for review and there are almost always ways of improving how you are doing something. Continuing improvement though, not change for the sake of it.

Question 3 is straightforward. You might have over- or underestimated timings. The involvement of others might have created blocks which you don't really have much control over. Sometimes you have to flex. If you're running two or more development areas at the same time, you can usually manage to progress with one while you're waiting for a response to the others.

Question 4 is picking up on the ongoing review mentioned in the introduction to the format page. Review how you stand. Are things going as you intended? Is your path progressing as you want it to? Is the content of the learning programme meeting your needs? Keep worrying away at it like a dog with a bone until you smooth out the raw edges.

Question 5 focuses on any blocks you've experienced.

Question 6 asks you to try to evaluate your own progress. How do you judge whether you're 'more competent'? Having specific objectives helps, as we've seen. With production, you can judge by productivity or output. In what always seems a rather negative way, you can judge by reductions in the number of complaints. In some of the soft skills, like dealing with customers or communication, it's perhaps more down to gut feelings. Give them a score out of 10 and they sound more scientific straight away! Evaluation's not an end in itself – it's so that you can do something to improve performance from that point onwards. This leads into Question 7.

Questions 8 and 9 are charting the way ahead. Having reviewed your progress to date, you are ready to move forward with renewed vigour. Questions 8 and 9 chart out your route map for the journey.

Format 12 (Appendix, page 226)

This is the formal document which you may need to submit for your personnel files, if you're involved in some type of formal continuing professional development (CPD). For this reason, it's set out in a fairly formal way – fear not, all will be explained!

Statement 1 is a statement of your key objective. We covered writing objectives in Chapter 5 so there shouldn't be too much of a problem with this one.

Statement 2 gives you descriptions of the outcomes of the exercise. Think in actions; think in terms of things that you are now competent at doing, as a direct result of your activities. Things such as, 'I am now competent at:

- discussing the key issues of the new policy
- operating the new piece of equipment
- completing all stages of the XYZ process
- reaching decisions based on stated legislation'.

Statement 3 is an opportunity for you to show that you have applied new or different activities and understand their applications and effects.

Statement 4 may or may not be relevant to any particular activity. The point here is that you are also developing yourself when you are involved in developing others, both from the use of communication and learning transfer techniques and also potentially through learning new information. So, being a mentor or coach for someone else's professional development can also count towards your own.

Everything needs evidence nowadays. **Statement 5** is where you log it. Evidence is any practical or physical action or thing which can be recorded: contracts achieved ; complimentary letters received; reports written; certificates awarded; projects completed (or progressed to a specific point). Anything which can be seen and noted as a positive record of development.

Statement 6 may be relevant – it is recording the 'bigger picture' again. How these outcomes tie in with others – and their overall importance.

Remember, Format 12 is unique in the planning system as being designed for handing over to someone else when completed. It is an official record, if you like. All the others – including the ones which follow on from this – are for your benefit, first and foremost. Never forget that.

Format 12 completes the sequence for that particular development area. The whole of this *ID Plan* sequence (Formats 6–12) will be repeated – or indeed can be running parallel at the same time – for one or more other Development Areas.

Format 13 (Appendix, page 227)

Personal development is more than just getting better at doing things. It also involves things such as:

- being more aware of what is going on around you
- caring for the environment – actively
- making opportunities to help others
- developing your home life positively
- putting something back into the community
- looking after your health – and the health of others
- working together with others – co-operatively

- expanding your spiritual awareness comfortably
- respecting the spiritual and moral beliefs of others.

I could go on but you get the picture – the bigger picture. This is going much further than training plans and achieving competencies. But it is an important part of becoming a 'better person'. That's part of the deal when you're thinking co-operatively. Remember – 'not stepping on the heads of other climbers when getting to the top of the mountain'. Using assertion in a positive way, to add your skills and knowledge to the co-operation pile, without trying to overshadow everyone else. Become part of the whole – but a bigger and more productive part.

What we're trying to do is integrate personal and professional development. Apply co-operative thinking to work better with others. Apply the holistic philosophy which has been presented throughout this book. 'Do as you would be done by.'

As with some of the early exercises in the book, it's first impressions that count in this format. They're not trick questions. There's no-one checking over your shoulder, ready to mock or question your beliefs. This is for your own benefit, to help you clarify your own ideas and values. So, ask yourself each question and record what you think first of all, as your real thoughts on the matter.

Question 1 is straightforward – don't analyse too deeply, just respond.

We've given some thought to work/life balance and we will be returning to the subject in the next chapter. You should be aware enough to respond – are you working too long? Is your home/family life as you'd like it? Do you have a comfortable transfer of skills between the two, helping the balance? **Question 2** can record your thoughts.

Question 3 is a simple question. Try to come up with a positive answer. You may already be involved in helping society in some way. If so, note it down.

Question 4 is a prompt to think carefully about personal stress. You may not be experiencing any, but if you are, do you have any thoughts on how you may be able to control things better, if necessary?

A large part of co-operation and being aware of others is trying to work with them and help them. Co-operation is a two-way process, however, so it's perfectly all right to seek help. Think of it as a more personal or even spiritual level of mentoring. From your various networking thoughts, you should have some potential contacts to note under **Question 5**. Don't forget your nearest and dearest as well – some people may be happier talking about personal matters with close family rather than a more impersonal counsellor. On the other hand, some may prefer the impersonal counsellor. Make your own decisions.

Question 6 is a bit of a mind jogger. Bigger picture thinking is encouraged through a broader view of what is going on in the world – and I mean the world, not your local area or the TV soaps. If you can't think of three current areas of concern, it's time to check the quality newspapers or watch the international news on TV.

Question 7 is the other side of the coin from Question 5. It's co-operative thinking time again. You've probably already thought of some names, so jot them down here.

Some people get a bit jumpy when they see the word 'spiritual'. A heightened awareness of the 'bigger picture' will almost automatically create a greater spiritual awareness in the person, whether it is a mainstream religious belief or belief in some overlying energy or presence. The more you think about it and talk to others about it, the more your beliefs and level of understanding and experience will clarify and consolidate and ultimately develop.

If you feel uneasy about **Question 8**, just leave it just now – but do try coming back to it periodically, as your personal and professional development continues to progress. At some point, it will be the right time to set your thoughts down.

Question 9 is straightforward. Don't think too hard – just go with the flow and write.

Format 14 (Appendix, page 228)

This is a combination of an Action Plan and a 'Things to Do' list. Nothing new – but very useful. It can be used in a variety of ways and ties in with the objectives, milestones and priorities we have already reviewed in great detail. Print off lots of copies and use it freely.

Format 15 (Appendix, page 229)

This is the extra 'bridge' sheet, to complete and use as you think fit, if you feel there are any gaps in the system. It's up to you – so you'll have to work out your own directions!

Summary

Using a development planning system will certainly help you keep firmer control over your journey through life and work. Regular and ongoing reviews of:

- activities
- priorities
- progress
- amendments
- reactions
- attitudes
- opportunities
- objectives
- outcomes

will provide both focus and balance.

It's finding the best balance point between work and life – the one which suits you – that is our quest now.

11 Finding my work/life balance point

Work/life balance is like a pendulum. It's a personal thing, with no catch-all solution to meet every need. It runs much deeper than basic considerations about working flexitime or job-sharing and sometimes founders because it can be quite difficult to organize and manage effectively. The acceptable balance point for my work/life pendulum is undoubtedly different from yours – but the options from which we select will be similar. So, let's look at some of these.

Work out time-24

- Is money more important to you than a flexible life-style?
- Is family/personal life more important than career progression?
- Are business travel perks more important than a regular home life?
- Are workmate relationships more important than those with friends?
- Is opulent retirement more important than enjoyment of your working day?
- Would you accept internal promotion regardless of where it was located?
- Which would you attend: your child's school play debut – or an evening business meeting?
- Do you prefer to manage stress physically/chemically – or live a more balanced life?
- Are you likely to take a day off in the sun, or hope the weather holds for the weekend?
- Do you feel in control of your future – or do you take care to keep on the right side of the decision-makers?

There are no right answers for these questions – it is entirely personal. The answers you choose will almost certainly vary with time. You've doubtless heard the expression 'making sacrifices' which implies straightaway that we're doing something other than that which we really want to do. But it can also imply that it's happening this time round, rather than always. Most working parents have missed out on attending some key event in their child's life and development. It's when your child has turned 14 and you realize that in the last performance you saw, he or she was third camel in the infant nativity play that you should wonder what's gone wrong – badly wrong!

Identifying your priorities

Work/life balance options will vary with the type of life you choose overall. And never lose sight of the fact that it is you who is choosing. But also bear in mind that your decisions will affect others, so consult and discuss. This is especially true for your home/life issues, if these will be shared with partners, family and others. Where change is in the air, the need for support is mutual – so talk through the pros and cons, and the implications before rushing off into the development sunset!

As you read each format page in your *ID Plan* your choices will be influenced by your personal work/life priorities. When you respond to each question in any single format, you are selecting the stance, which leads to the action, which results in the outcome – to best suit your own balance preferences.

Your ability – and degree of success – in getting the balance right does, of course, depend on the flexibility and control which you personally have over your working day. Work/life balance will also be influenced by your domestic situation, perhaps especially if you are the parent of a young child. There will always be some degree of influence you can apply, however.

Consider the different priorities of the following:

■ a working parent
■ a single working parent

- a self-employed individual – with further considerations if home-working
- a conventional nine-to-five business employee
- a business employee where late/extra working is expected/ demanded
- a job-sharing employee, paired with another to jointly meet goals
- a hard up, part-time worker on (near) minimum wage
- an ex-pat. contract worker with a family back in the country of residence
- an employee (e.g. forces) where there are extended work/social activities.

You can probably think of other permutations. You will currently fall into at least one and possibly several of these categories. It is quite possible that your career path will take you through several of these different categories, and you will probably be happier with some than others. 'Life', as they say, 'is a learning experience.' So, of course, is 'Work'. But it's important that we do learn. Don't get stuck in the one path – or indeed the one track – for reasons such as money or status, if it really is messing up the way you live, or your overall health. You do have the choice.

So, if there are so many options, permutations and personal priorities, how can we possibly come up with checklists which can help you complete your planning formats and thus solve your work/life dilemmas? With great difficulty! But it's worth a try.

You've already considered angles on work/life balance in Chapter 6 – check back to *FIND OUT Time 16* (page 101) and *WORK OUT Time 17* (page 108) if you need to refresh your memory. You've also been thinking about some of the decisions and priorities which may be important to you, when we were working through the different *ID Plan* formats, especially Formats 11 and 13, so the ideas are already there.

Visualize your path on the track with the milestones behind you and those stretching forward towards the horizon. How sure are you that this path into the future will give you the kind of work/life balance you really want? How ready are you to amend your plans as you progress if necessary, to match your changing priorities? Let's see.

Find out time-22

1 Do you enjoy doing what you are doing every day?

2 How could you improve it?

3 Do you look forward to your home life each evening?

4 How could you improve it?

5 Do you reach Sunday evening with things you want to do still unfinished?

6 Which elements of your total existence cause you stress?

7 How could you relieve this?

8 Can you make good use of – and develop – your life skills at work?

9 What extra opportunities would be valuable?

10 Can you make good use of – and develop – your work skills in your general life?

---

11 What additional avenues could you seek out to apply these more?

---

12 What's your number one priority for your personal work/life balance?

Think through your responses to these 12 questions, then visualize your path and milestones again. Are there any potential changes which come to mind?

Achieving the balance takes time

A recurring theme in this book has been the extending time element. If you want something to happen – really want it, that is – it will happen. But it may take a lot longer than you would initially have expected or wanted. In order for it to happen, it will need your involvement. That's not fate, or good luck or even assertiveness. It's down to keeping a clear focus, with regular revisiting of the milestones to make sure you're still heading in your chosen direction. And you're also checking that the way you have selected was not only initially correct but is holding up to the scrutiny of experience. If it doesn't, are you objective – and ego-free – enough to step back, see the bigger picture and review and revise your journey? Forward planning your route does not commit you to a certain path regardless. It's helped you review the options in reaching the decision to take that path, so you are better prepared to come up with an alternative 'Plan B' option rapidly, if the need arises.

So, sorting out your balance point may extend over a much longer period of time than you would initially have thought, especially if progress has to 'go on hold' while you wait for some delay to unblock. In this situation, work/life balance goes much deeper than time allocations in your working week. We're looking at complex choices here, including:

- job (and life) satisfaction
- general reduction in and control of stress
- availability of quality time (with family/social/work colleagues, etc)
- potential for future development (work and life issues)
- the chance to apply work skills in life and vice versa
- having the organization in place to make it happen.

Let's consider an example.

Work out time-25

Consider the following steps and stages of work/career development, with associated life balance considerations. In order to be able to expand on the balance aspects, I have chosen my own direct experience – I hope you can indulge me with this one bit of personal focus!

Once you have considered my pros and cons, you can then consider your own parallels.

1   I started working life as a qualified teacher, with a particular interest in educational technology, at this stage more the equipment than the structural theories. I hated the discipline side of teaching children but enjoyed working with learning hardware and software. I didn't enjoy spending my evenings marking workbooks and preparing lessons.

Overall, I disliked my work, which caused me some degree of stress. I compensated by taking an interest in developing educational resources, running a mobile discotheque, folk singing and a range of outside 'life balances', which outweighed my work interest heavily.

2   I became a lecturer in educational technology in a London college, involved in both lecturing and practical tutoring for teachers. I enjoyed this greatly, even though it involved many evening hours preparing lesson plans and resources. With our first child born and a single salary, we found living in London too expensive, causing some financial strains.

I enjoyed this work with adults and, although I spent many hours of my home life preparing lessons, I didn't resent it, as previously. Tight finances restricted 'life' activities and made it necessary for me to seek a higher salary. The balance had swung towards me spending more time on work activities.

3   I was then employed as an educational technology adviser in a Glasgow centre. Due to political reasons relating to local authority reorganization, this turned out to be a really bum job, with much stress associated with poor management relationships and lack of career challenge. I focused more on home life, largely to blank out the frustrations at work.

I was under-employed at work, with little scope to expand my capabilities and general frustration when I attempted to expand ideas. I masked the stress associated with this by arranging education-based exhibitions in the centre when I could and swinging my balance strongly towards home life.

4   My next position was as manager of a learning and resources centre in Hampshire. This involved setting up new premises and developing resources, with a staff of 10. I enjoyed this greatly, with responsibility for my own workload for the first time – as well as enjoying family life. I achieved most of my goals in five years and decided to move into business training.

As I am motivated by the challenge of responsibility and workload flexibility, my preferred work/life balance was largely achieved in this job, combined with a busy family/home life. With the new centre established, I moved on naturally to seek a greater challenge within business.

5   As a senior consultant with a training provider in London, I was motivated by the ever-continuing challenge of an expanding course portfolio. This again involved a lot of evening preparation time but I enjoyed it overall. Much of my home life was spent on refurbishing our house, plus family life – giving a work/life balance which was acceptable, if exhausting.

I found the business world stimulating, which compensated for the high pressure of delivering a full course programme. With home life also stimu-lating (although the additional DIY work was quite exhausting,) this gave a good overall work/life balance, although unsustainable for too long a time.

6   My next role was setting up an international training function for an Amer-ican multinational, based in Brussels. With complete control of the work-load and international travel, coupled with a wonderful family life and European travel at weekends, this was probably my high point in work/life balance. Sadly, the parent company closed down the function after 2+ years.

This position, with the mix of work challenge, development and personal control coupled with domestic enjoyment and flexibility (it was a rented house so no DIY was required!) provided a high level of work/life balance. Closure over the final six-month period, with many training events pre-arranged, was evidently dissatisfying but even this involvement gave an acceptable degree of balance.

7   My subsequent self-employed, home-office based consultancy status has varied in both areas of specialization and volume of work. With house moves from London to Wiltshire to Scotland, this has changed domestic life and priorities dramatically. The work/life balance is a more flexible issue now – with some large percentage of my time involved in writing books, scripts and articles (which hardly feels like work at all!).

As self-employed and working to self-imposed deadlines, there have been times when I work too long into the evenings – but equally I can take com-

plete or part days off when I feel like it, to enjoy home life or get involved in
non-work activities. The balance is controllable, as long as assignments
continue. This situation currently gives me an almost-total influence and
control over my work/life balance.

So, there's a thumbnail sketch of my life – it's a lot more complex than that
but I hope to have illustrated that:

- some situations give greater control of work/life balance than others
- as with time management, you need some control over your work/life priorities
- you can select a path which progressively gives you what you value most
- where you've made an error of judgement, dust yourself down and proceed
- it's worth refining your direction to provide the opportunities you prefer
- opportunities will arise in the future which will encourage balance adjustments
- being clear on your strengths and priorities helps you maintain progress.

Spend a little time looking back over your work/life progress so far and try to
judge how satisfied you are with the way things have developed. Be as objective as you can – this is for your eyes only – it may well give you a deeper
insight into what really makes you tick. It might also give you some indicators
as to how you would really like to redesign the rest of your life.

You can do it, over time, if the focus is there. Brilliant focus – brilliant future. Getting the correct balance does take time and will possibly involve a degree of trial and error. On occasion, a situation which should have provided balance in theory doesn't work out because of politics, personalities or differing priorities. Sometimes, the situation can be resolved with negotiation; at other times, it's better to look to new horizons. But remember, don't close one door before you see another open in front of you. This helps control the stress and self-doubt that can otherwise threaten.

Different balances for different lifestyles

Earlier in this chapter, we thought about some of the different work/life balance options – part-time, full-time, parent, self-employed and so on.

If you're a full-time (sheep) worker, struggling to find enough 'lifetime', the flexibility of self-employment can seem very attractive. Being self-employed (goat), however, you can find yourself with too much free time if you have a mortgage and other financial commitments to meet. In self-employment, time really is money. Unless you're involved in one of the self-employed trades where your services aways seem to be in great demand, being under-employed for extended periods of time can certainly tarnish the gleam of self-employment. It takes time to get used to the ups and downs, so that you can enjoy your free times, knowing confidently that you will be working and earning again soon. The ever-changing attitudes and priorities of society and the natural bell curve of average business success and progress don't help either. Because of – or despite – all these elements, it's a full-time journey heading towards that balance point of work/life contentment. And planning and monitoring that journey requires the help of a good personal planning system, to keep you focused.

It gets worse if you're unemployed, of course. You can find yourself really resenting all these lucky people travelling into work each day. It's a strange world! The apparent glamour of early retirement can even pale slightly, with some individuals struggling to come to terms with the realization that they will never apply their skills again. But then, of course they can. This is another element of work/life balance, with skills being ploughed back into helping the community. Everyone benefits. Retired accountants or business secretaries 'doing the books' for the local sports clubs; retired tradesmen helping out with repairs to the community hall or scout hut; retired teachers chairing local societies – the list can go on and on.

Think of work/life balance as an ever-flexible continuing process. Not so much a set of weighing scales as one of those bamboo water features in a Zen garden, filling up – reaching the point of balance – overflowing – unbalancing – gradually filling up again, and so on, but never stressed, always responsive and peaceful. As the saying goes 'Life is a journey, not a destination', but it sure helps if you have some idea of the correct direction and some control over your means and pace of travel!

Finding a correct work/life balance can also involve levels of responsibility, with major extremes often there for all to see. Can you think of any individuals who freewheel through their job, doing only as much as is necessary to get by without upsetting things – then spring to life during the evenings and weekends when they become totally absorbed in their hobby or outside interest? Work is seen as primarily there to earn enough to exist, while financing the hobby. And that's fine, it works for them and the world of administration would be a poorer place without them.

At the other extreme, there are people who live for their work, continuing well into the evening by choice rather than necessity. Somewhere around the middle is the old 'salaryman' attitude we come across in Japanese business, where the working day is governed artificially by the time when the boss decides to go home. Subordinates sit around, not daring to be the 'tall poppy' who leaves work first, although not necessarily being very productive while they wait. This evening attendance, which can sometimes extend further to 'team bonding' sessions in the bar, has an obvious effect on domestic life and work/life balances. That's why the Japanese wife invariably rules the home and incidentally, chooses the family car (one reason why the interior finish in Japanese models is so good). By current Western standards, this 'jacket on the back of the chair' syndrome is perhaps seen as a poor goal to strive towards – but there are schools of thought which equate it with productivity.

What is the difference between:

- motivation towards higher productivity *and*
- achieving a sustainable work/life balance?

This is akin to the search for the Holy Grail – find the answer, bottle it and wealth will be yours!

The clue perhaps is in the word 'sustainable'. Think of motor manufacturing, with the car production line moving forward relentlessly at a pre-set rate. Think of the call centres proliferating around the country, with their flashing displays of volume of unanswered calls waiting. Think of any work situation where 'productivity' is gradually, persistently trying to get more out of less.

Think basic work/life balancing and the simple solution is part-time working. Find the optimum length of time that you can push the average worker to greater heights each week, then employ as many as necessary for as short a period as necessary to keep the seat warm for the complete week. Good for business; good for the unemployment figures, and it gives the workers lots of free time, right?

Well, wrong, actually. If they can find it, many are holding down several part-time jobs to fill their week, in order to earn enough money to live (and perhaps pay the child minder so that the mother can work even longer hours). Each job extracting the maximum effort, potentially leading to exhaustion, stress and a hollow home life. Where's the work/life balance there?

Think about the following:

1   What are the three things that motivate you most about the work you do?

2 What are the three things you enjoy most about your home (non-work) life?

3 What two things take up too much of your time currently?

4 What two things would you like to spend more time doing?

5 What are your main goals towards giving you inner contentment?

6 How do you go about achieving these?

7 What single change would immediately improve your work/life balance?

8 What longer-term development would lead to a better work/life balance for yourself?

9 Which relationships could you develop to improve your work/life balance?

10 How would you describe your own perfect work/life balance?

Think about these ten questions for a while and note down your answers.
It will be time well spent – believe me!

In short, work/life balance is a complex idea. But worth thinking about.

Chill out time-20

Find a quiet corner where you won't be disturbed for a while.

Think back to the previous chapter and focus on those *ID Plan* formats which perhaps pressed your whoopee button – the key issues which could direct your brilliant future.

Look back at the notes of your responses to the exercises in this chapter. Figure out your direction at the moment with regard to reaching a work/life balance and review what you still have to do to get it moving smoothly.

Focus on the two or three things you reckon you have to do first of all.

Work out a plan of action.

Think about it for a while and smooth off some of the rough edges.

Check through your *ID Plan* format pages and select the relevant questions and sections.

Respond to these to give you your next steps and stages.

You're on the way to your brilliant future!

12 Holistic horizons

You'll be setting out all on your own shortly but that's fine. You're ready. Just don't rush off too fast at the start – and keep one eye on the milestones ahead!

Work out time-26

It's bigger picture time.

If you haven't already done it, copy the 15 *ID Plan* formats from the website *www.business-minds.com*, Brilliant Future section. They're available as reduced copies in the appendix of this book – but you'll have greater flexibility with them as separate sheets.

Now, spread them out in the correct sequence on a flat surface. The floor will do if you don't have a large table, as long as you can manage to crawl around on the floor!

There's the complete planning system – you're looking at the scope for setting out your brilliant future – and working it through, step by step. You've studied them individually and had first thoughts about things that work for you and others that don't. Now, get the 'big picture' handle on the whole thing and see how you can move on down your path.

Really think about it. Overview the whole system and play around with the options a bit, thinking real examples, real possibilities. Identify the ones you see as more valuable – for your immediate priorities anyway. The others will have their uses later, don't worry. They're all there to help you. The future's brilliant, if you make it happen.

OK. So you've got a mental picture of the planning system in your mind's eye and of how it's likely to work for you.

The next bit of visualization involves you. You've done it before, several times, throughout the book. This is the climax. Live it.

You are the spark of energy at the head of your path, down there on the development track. It's your path that you see trailing behind – just look at some of these meanderings. But you're still progressing well and the pace is about to rack up dramatically.

What we need to do now is check out the various milestones along your path – make sure the focus is there. It will make the *ID Plan* work; it will help you progress; it will make the world a better place, in some small (or large) way. Let's go for it.

Milestone 1: Look to the future

Think in different time frames. One of the main points in using a planning system is that capturing the information and plans for the future will free your mind to focus on the *now*. What it is you have to do *now*, to make things happen *now*. But not in isolation. Your judgements will be coloured – positively coloured, not clouded by grudges – by things that have happened in the past. And they will be influenced by the destination you've chosen for yourself. This is where forward planning becomes so useful.

Learn from the past – but leave it behind. Forget it. Focus on the *now* and look to the future. But be flexible. Life changes. Priorities change – some you can influence, sure, but with others, just go with the flow. You can only change the world so much – don't let the frustrations around grind you down. Flex your future plans to help yourself, while at the same time helping others. Think co-operation, not aggressive assertion.

I D Plan will help you map out your brilliant future – and help you make it happen in the best way possible, given all the circumstances that surround you. Work with it, but be selective; it's a tool to help you, not bog you down in writing for its own sake.

Think carefully about the questions and your responses – your future rests on them.

Milestone 2: Sort through your priorities

Everything's important – but some things are more important than others.

If you're doing a job and you lose a favourite tool – a screwdriver, pen or whatever – do you waste minutes/hours searching for it, or do you find a substitute and get on with the job? The favourite tool will always turn up, usually when you're tidying up after finishing! Sometimes, you really need that specific tool – you can't complete the job without it. OK, that's different – stop everything and go seek. But keep an open mind and view these priorities objectively.

Remember your 'things to do' lists. That's prioritization in action. Priorities shift – move with them. Remember the tall poppy flexing in the wind. Nothing's that important in life. Think big picture. What's the big deal with a delay in having a meal when some of the world's population is starving, literally starving. What's the problem with waiting a few months to develop your career in a particular direction, when there are millions around the world who will *never* have a real job.

Everything is on a sliding scale. Everything is relative. Go with the flow but remain focused. Revisit your planning system regularly and review those priorities. There will always be ways of moving something forward. Ultimately, most things will progress and if the occasional thing bogs down in the mud and sinks from view, it's not the end of the world. There are lots of positive options open for you – seek them out.

Milestone 3: Set off down your path

Ultimately, you've got to go for it. Planning is there to give you the route map and help you figure out some of the possible hazards and what you can do about them. But the path's real, not virtual, so you've got to get mud on your boots. Little steps and big steps – but striding off down the path as confidently as you can.

You're trying to keep your path running in as straight a line as possible but accept that flexibility will create twists and turns. Not a problem. Use your forward planning to anticipate; be ready for the blocks and delays, but also the opportunities. It works both ways – if you're prepared. Remember that both the negative and the positive connections of a battery are necessary to get the energy flowing.

The *ID Plan* system will give you the steps and stages, the resources and contacts, leaving you to concentrate on the path ahead and giving you the clear head and the confidence to move at the best pace you can, in the circumstances. And never forget that you're sharing the track with others. Network, discuss, enquire, listen – the information and help are out there.

Milestone 4: Choose your mode of travel

'Horses for courses', as they say. Horse, bike, car, quad, 4×4, truck, argocat, hovercraft, boat, there are many ways of getting from A to B. There are equally many ways to learn new information; many techniques to apply for your personal and professional development. Some will suit each situation better than others; some will suit your individual needs better than others. Choose carefully.

Don't settle for the easy option. Don't just use the resource that comes easily to hand, whether it is course, textbook or e-learning. Be selective. Be discerning. Read the objectives and the expected outcomes. Match them with your needs. If you know what you're looking for, you'll know when you've found it. And you'll know how to use it – effectively.

And don't settle for the same method of travelling – the same way of learning – all the time. Different subjects need different ways of getting the message across. Facts and instructions can be set out in lists and structures; activities require you to be doing things, not reading about them, or just listening to people talking about them. Learning how to work with people needs exercises in working with actual people. Real – not virtual. Get some mud on your boots. Different horses run best on specific courses. Think what the saying actually means, in a racing context. It works for humans too!

The same goes if you're selecting from a range of resources or learning events. If you're clear what your own goal is, you can match the outcomes set out for the various resources against your own objectives. And if there's a package or programme which doesn't state its objectives or outcomes, don't waste your time with it. There are plenty of good resources out there – don't be dazzled by the technology or the glitzy packaging. Be selective. Be objective.

Milestone 5: Seek out assistance

Remember the triangle: yourself, the range of coaches and mentors available and the support from training and resources providers. This is an integrated triangle, gradually building momentum. Use it. Encourage it to develop. Put something into it as well as taking something out. Every learner's a potential mentor/coach.

Assistance comes differently for sheep-types within an organization than for more independent goat-types. You have to seek it in different ways. The established HR department as well as the enterprise and skills councils and commercial companies. The formal provider as well as the informal networker. The organized course as well as the *ad hoc* workplace assistance.

Think objectively. Be as clear as possible in your mind about what it is you're looking for before you set off on your quest. Time is money. If you're asking a favour from someone, they may be happy to help you but not to stand around waiting for you to figure out what it is you want. Be flexible and fit into people's schedules. Don't expect instant responses. And, if you can do all that, you'll be amazed how helpful people can be.

There's a vast resource of people out there who are potentially mentors and coaches – including you – if the correct atmosphere can be created. Work at it, it's certainly worth the effort. You'll need some help, certainly. That's where the development support or Training/Personnel Department comes into play, certainly for sheep-types. The help should be there, if you ask for it. It may take time. It may be slow to develop, initially. But once the successes become apparent, visible, tangible, then the whole thing should begin to take off. The integrated triangle begins to revolve. Remember the Catherine Wheel? 360° mentoring in action. Let it happen – make it happen.

Milestone 6: Think co-operation

Belonging; assertion; co-operation. It's all part of a gradual progress. Work with it. Break through the initial barriers of suspicion which can be there – be genuine; be honest; be positive. It pays dividends, certainly in the long run but very often in the short term as well.

'Why is this guy offering to help? What's in it for him? What's he trying to con me into doing?'

'Well, maybe nothing. Maybe he just feels like helping. Because somebody else helped him last week. And maybe it will encourage you to help somebody else next week.'

And so co-operation grows.

Think about it. Think bigger picture. Think longer term. You don't have to repay directly, helpfulness grows and flourishes, like thistledown in the wind.

It's that holistic thing. The overall outcome being worth more than the little bits which you are adding together. If an atmosphere of helpfulness develops, the overall atmosphere begins to buzz. You have the energy – you have lift-off.

Milestone 7: Think flexibility

Keep an open mind. Don't get stuck in a rut. There will be blockages, remember your path. You may prefer life to go in a straight line but it seldom does. Accept the bends and meanderings. This is where future planning, considering the options and knowing the field ahead all help you cope with changes of pace and direction.

Look down onto the track. Visualize all the other paths, the other little sparks of energy going about the progress of their daily lives and career development. Sometimes, these paths will run side by side – team up with others doing the same thing. Benefit from each other's experience. Sometimes the lines will cross – you may even get in each other's way. Be patient. Think positive. Sometimes, you might even meet someone passing you, going back the way you have come, puzzled, confused, lost. Give them a helping hand to get back on course again. It won't do you any harm – and someone might do the same for you in the future, if the atmosphere's right. It's your positive actions which help create this atmosphere.

Think positive. OK, there will always be the occasional selfish individual, taking and never giving. But that's no reason for others to act in the same way. Lead by example. Others might even learn – and change their ways – through our example. It certainly helps to think positively.

Aim for flexibility in the way you do things; flexibility in the way you develop. Be flexible in the way you deal with people; be flexible in the way you plan your future.

Milestone 8: Get the message across

Keep thinking big picture. Keep asking yourself what you are really trying to do; what you're really trying to achieve. Keep the focus, sell the key points without getting bogged down in the detail. Think of a good communicator – what is it that you admire about the way they tell it? Identify and bottle. That's what you can use. Refine your message, to get as many potential ideas out in the open as you can. But keep them clear and uncluttered with extra baggage. Keep to the point.

Focus your mind before you discuss – make notes if it helps. Being specific helps you get the message across – and provides you with the help you need. This is where planning helps. Be the great communicator.

Milestone 9: Be aware of the scope available

The options are there if you look for them. Once you've established your milestones ahead, the future path becomes clearer. Speak to people; read widely; listen when being told about possibilities. And make notes if it helps.

The scope can vary. Once you've found a source that has done a certain thing in the past – work on it. It may not be quite the thing you're looking for. The course may have slightly different objectives and priorities, for example; the individual may not have had quite the correct experience. But the scope can often grow from there. There may be a specialist course, or modules from the course, which you can use instead; the individual might have had the additional experience you seek – or know someone else who has. Networking is a chain reaction – it's amazing the number of people who 'know a man who does', even if they don't do it themselves.

There's always new information to find out; there are always new sources to make a note of, for current or future use. The more you've planned possible routes ahead, the broader your scope for identifying support when the need arises.

Milestone 10: Get people involved

You're an individual learner. What can you do to involve others? Is it your role to do it actually? Well – why not? You don't get if you don't ask. But ask nicely, co-operatively.

Thinking in terms of an integrated triangle is a fresh concept. If the support's there – if the company or whatever is really wanting it to happen – it needs total involvement. Informal mentoring, coaching and other types of support need as much enthusiasm as possible. They also need a bit of training to make sure the focus and structure are there. So the involvement's from the top initially, with some organization to make sure that the same route map's being used by everyone. Not forcing everyone along the same path, saying the same things, carrying the same loads. People are individuals and, in the informal sense we're picturing, need a bit of slack to develop in the way they want. To develop in their own preferred way as learners as well as mentors. It all helps keep the motivation going – keeps that old whoopee factor alive and well and singing in your heart.

You're building a structure based on co-operation. People are doing it because they want to do it and not because they have to. However, if you mess them around, they won't want to continue. Treat them like sensible, helpful individuals and flex to fit in with their needs as well as your own and the co-operation can grow. Remember the time factor: you sometimes have to wait – but things will ultimately happen if you continue to want them to. Sometimes over time you'll change your mind – perhaps priorities change; perhaps your needs alter. Don't waste your time and that of others by carrying on down alleys you know are blind. Get access to the learning you need, when you need it. There's no point in going on a course which only starts six months after your learning need's been identified. It's better to get some input now. There's got to be an internal mentor or coach who can help you along your path now. Only this can get you moving in the correct direction again. The mentor/coaches are out there – it's just a matter of finding them and getting them involved. You may still benefit from the formal course later, when it's scheduled, but then again, you might already be up and running, thanks to your informal mentoring and loads of direct, reinforced experience. *ID Plan* formats will help you identify all the detail you need to know to get that experience and head on down your development path.

Milestone 11: Check and refine your path

You are a living being. The world you live in is alive, dynamic, changing. You are working and living with other people who are constantly changing as individuals. Subtly, perhaps, but the changes are there. And, holistically, your actions and interactions with them create an overwhelming atmosphere which ebbs and flows, like the tides and currents of the sea. Things never stand still. Plans are never carved in stone. They're made to be revisited, refined, updated. But, in doing this, they keep your progress dynamic and responsive, cutting down on the number of blocks which could hold up your journey.

Don't feel that, when you've set down your future development plans in your *ID Plan* system, it's the end of the process. It's only the beginning. Any system which is working and interacting with loads of other individuals like yourself is bound to be flexible. You wouldn't wish for anything less. But you've got the basic path to work from. You've got your key focus. Hold it. Work on it. Refine it.

And, if you get a major shift of view – you decide that your future direction and development should really be going down the left rather than the right fork at this crossroads – you'll have to review your plans in the light of this. But that's fine too. It's better than carrying on grudgingly down the expected route, thinking 'if only'. Don't allow yourself to reach the end of your active life, this time round anyway, still wishing you had managed to do something. If you want it that badly, make it happen, even if only in some small way. Maybe you won't write a best seller – but you can produce copy for the local press or a script for the community pantomime. Maybe you won't be a champion athlete – but you can be an active member of your local games team, for football, rugby, hockey, squash, shinty or whatever, and achieve a huge amount of enjoyment in the process.

Milestone 12: Develop yourself personally

This is the spiritual side of the equation – using the term in the widest way. It's the big questions: Why are you here? What do you want to do with your life? How do you want to develop to be a 'better person'? What indeed do we mean by 'being a better person'? How can we raise our level of consciousness – and what are we becoming more conscious of? Can we look more deeply into ourselves, in order to understand ourselves better? And, if we can see who we are and where we'd like to be going, can we then maintain both the focus and drive to keep progressing?

Much of the development we have been thinking about throughout this book has been about developing our work and career. But implicit in all this – in our work/life balance, our dealings with others and in our choice of priorities – we are also trying to build a better, more open and co-operative way of life, creating a higher level of understanding of ourselves and what we are trying to achieve. We've also been trying to link the two threads of personal and more work-related professional development together into some acceptable balance point. It's not necessarily a religious thing – but it is a way of thinking which is helped by having some consciousness of a driving force or energy out there which keeps the whole thing moving forward dynamically. It's certainly a holistic thing, where individual sparks of energy can gradually build together to create the almost limitless burning flame of positive progress.

There's a principle called 'the hundred monkeys principle'. It's also called 'critical mass'. In any progress, any movement towards change and development, there is some trigger point. You can have a few individuals trying to make what they see as a positive change to society but they can easily be shouted down or laughed out of court. In the animal kingdom, the few monkeys may be initially screeched down by the rest of the pack. But if they, or you, persevere, you will usually find a few more individuals support the viewpoint, then a few more. Then there will be others who believe similar things in a different town, or a different country, who will network together. The internet makes the world a very compact place and before you know it, the hundred monkeys have gathered; the critical mass point has been reached. And the government or whoever is blocking progress can no longer turn a blind eye. Of course, there are different responses when it comes to this point, depending on levels of real democracy, but the world at large is aware of the call for change and things will never be quite the same again.

Never be afraid of being one of the hundred monkeys, or of being a tall poppy bending flexibly in the winds of change. Take your time. Maintain your focus. Flex with the pervailing moods of the moment and be ready to move forward when the atmosphere and opportunity become right. It will inevitably happen, eventually.

Whatever the personal development path you decide to follow, seek out the help and companionship of like-minded souls. In this form of journey, it is easier to travel in convoy. It gives you the strength, confidence and sometimes the protection you require. It gives you the scope to discuss, expand and develop your own thinking and gain exposure to additional, linked trains of thought. And it gives you the co-operation of companionship which can mean so much when you're struggling with difficult concepts and relationships. It's sometimes not easy to find like-minded people but they will appear, if you seek out the right events and situations and go out there and network, in whatever way you feel comfortable.

Milestone 13: Get that work/life balance right

Very important this, we've already considered it in some detail. It means different things to different people but you should see it in a much wider context than merely the number of hours you work each week and how much free time you have at home to bond with the family.

It's part of linking both personal and professional life and development together again, where each can build off applying the other in a parallel, positive way. Using some of your work skills for the good of the community, for example, or using your open and friendly skills for dealing with people generally, when you are liaising with work colleagues. But then, why should there be a difference in the way you respond to these two different groups of people? Conversely, do you treat your children differently from the way you would treat a work colleague?

Increasingly, people are weighing up the degree of influence which their work is having on their personal life. It was bound to happen as the shift kicked in against jobs for life and the caring parental attitude which some traditional companies used to have towards their employees. A company happy to 'let people go' through 'downsizing' and other such euphemisms cannot expect undying loyalty from their employees; companies offering one-year contracts cannot really expect employees to see a long-term future under their roof, although some do. And, in the buyers' market that is the employment of the moment, they can often get away with it. On the other hand, some employees will now consider very carefully whether they want to work away from home for long periods, uproot the family home for what might be a short period or be put in other similar situations where their life is being overwhelmingly influenced by their work. To some, being allowed to work from home helps the balance, while others see this as yet another encroachment of work into home life. If you don't like the way things are moving, look around quietly for something better or different. But don't close the door hastily, as you may live to regret it. Take your time, focus and find the new, better door to go through first.

This balance thing can work equally for the personal and professional sides of your development. In many ways, the two groupings are very similar. You should find it quite easy to apply some of your personal standards and skills in your professional life – and vice versa. Stay true to your values and try to incorporate the 'bigger picture' view into the way you're living your life overall. Work/life and personal/professional balances give an ongoing, flexible outlook on life which should encourage regular – almost continuous – review of your plans and progress. Keep an open mind – it keeps you on the right path.

Milestone 14: Inject the whoopee factor again

When did you last feel 'whoopee' about something you were doing? If it was longer than two weeks ago, what can you do about it? If you're clear about where you want to go, any major progress towards this should give you a buzz. If you're too tired to buzz, shouldn't you be looking at your work/life balance? If you don't see any progress now, or on the horizon, what one dynamic thing could you do to help? There must be something – really think about it!

Which parts of your work give you most satisfaction? Is there anything you've ever done in your life (or work) which has made you feel very emotional about how good it felt at that moment? That's what you want to re-create. Not artificially but by seeking out the things that make you feel good. Call it self-motivation or whatever. But it will get you buzzing again.

How would you choose to focus on yourself? Is it a case of a bit of pampering – an aromatherapy massage perhaps, a yoga session or a nice hot bath with candles, incense and essential oils? If the need is limited to an afternoon of retail therapy in the High Street, maybe you need to be viewing your life a little more holistically!

Anticipating a self-focus session should encourage the old whoopee feelings again. And having it should be one long, extended enjoyment. If what you do at work is close to your heart in any way, there should be similar experiences which give you deep enjoyment and satisfaction. Perhaps it's achieving something new, closing a sale, cracking a problem or working successfully to a team outcome. Think positively and the examples will pop up. Anticipate. Enjoy. *Whoopee.*

Milestone 15: Apply the *ID Plan* thoughtfully

You have the tools and you know how to use them – in principle anyway. The next stage is trying it out. As I've said, use it in a way that *you* find helpful and you'll see its benefits. Gradually, you'll use different formats in different ways to satisfy different development needs. That's what it's all about. Use it flexibly, to suit your own priorities. Don't ever get bogged down in the detail. If in doubt, leave it and move on to the next section. You can always return when things become clearer, as the plans evolve.

I D means *individual development* but also focuses on your chosen *identity*. It's all part of refining and progressing your path along the track. You can monitor and control this to some large extent yourself. But you're not alone. Always remember the integrated triangle – with all the potential support available, if you and others give it a chance. And with the personal – or spiritual, if you prefer – sides of your life, think hard about the ways you want to develop. Focus on people, nature, a better world, a cleaner environment, widespread peace, deeper interactions with others at a higher level of understanding. There are many things to focus on as you go forward in life. 'Here are some which I prepared earlier', as the saying goes – you may want to consider them for a quiet moment or two. Think of it as a special – a very special – *CHILL OUT Time*. I hope you find it meaningful enough to return to read afresh from time to time.

Twenty tenets for a more holistic way of life

- Build positive thought.

- Be aware of yourself and others.

- Believe in yourself and others.

- Act as selflessly as you can.

- Allow time to do things properly.

- Give matters time to evolve.

- Allow yourself 'Chill Out' times for thinking.

- Rest, relax and focus (meditate).

- Use visualization to concentrate thought.

- Observe and learn from world affairs and history.

- Work towards co-operation and away from egocentricity.

- Consider the effects of your actions.

- Apply holistic thinking when the time seems appropriate.

- Do what ultimately feels right.

- Reduce your dependence on stimulants and medication.

- Believe in the healing power of positive thought.

- Exercise in as natural an environment as possible.

- Retain an overview of the bigger picture.

- Maintain a focused view of your development path.

- Amend your plans flexibly to maintain progress.

It's a lot to expect from a personal development system; it's a lot to expect from a single individual. It's a long path, with many milestones. But you can progress down that path to the best of your ability, using all the tools and competency that has been given to you. You may only get so far along the path this time around – but that's progress. Enjoy it. Feel that *whoopee* tingle again!

Milestone 16: Onwards and upwards

There's a lot to think about here. We're talking individual development but we're talking about the real world, with loads of unique individuals and lots of different ways of living and doing business. We're speaking about integrated triangles, while accepting the fact that some corners of some triangles will be buzzing more than others. We must also expect some triangles to be in better shape than others. We're speaking about change and progress, while acknowledging that some of it will take a long time, often involving a range of blocks and meanders along the way.

However, with maintained effort, regular and ongoing planning and a positive view towards life, you can make it happen, to the best of your ability. You will be clearer now about where you want to go – *ID Plan* will help you get there.

appendix

ID Plan

route maps

brilliant future

(Formats 1–15)

The following formats 1–15 are available on the web, on *www.business-minds.com/goto/bfplan*. These will allow you to data enter your information and responses before printing them off for reference. You can, of course, also print them off as blank formats for subsequent hand-written completion. These webpage formats will give you more space for data entry than the condensed versions which follow in this book appendix. If you choose to use copies of the book appendix sheets, you may need to use an extra notepad to expand your responses.

Format 1

ID Plan **Individual Planning System ....for a brilliant future.**
Strengths and Shortfalls

Name ....Date ....Ref ....

Write down your first impressions for the following – you can sort out priorities later.

1 My five main strengths are:

2 My five key shortfall areas are:

Looking back through these strengths and shortfalls:

- identify any you think would be very difficult for you to improve (*)
- number the remainder in order of importance to your future
  (1 = high).

3 For the top two of each, what methods would you like to use to develop these?

Strengths   Shortfalls
1   #1

#2   #2

4 Any ideas for compensating for any of your shortfall areas?

© Chris Sangster Development 2001

Format 2

ID Plan **Individual Planning System** ....**for a brilliant future.**
Specific Development Areas

Name ....Date ....Ref ....

From your notes on Format 1, write down headings for up to six
development areas which you want to work on over the next period of
time. For each area, note any ideas you have for ways of becoming more
competent in that area.
Once you have finished, give each a priority – with #1 = top priority.

Development Area A............................. Overall priority rating ....
Initial Action Notes

Development Area B.............................Overall priority rating ....
Initial Action Notes

Development Area C.............................Overall priority rating ....
Initial Action Notes

Development Area D.............................Overall priority rating ....
Initial Action Notes

Development Area E ....Overall priority rating ....
Initial Action Notes

Development Area F .... Overall priority rating ....
Initial Action Notes

© Chris Sangster Development 2001

Format 3

ID Plan **Individual Planning System** ....for a brilliant future.
SHEEP PLAN – Employee Development Routes

1 For specific development areas, note down any learning opportunities of which you are aware (perhaps supplied directly by or indirectly through your employer).

2 Are you aware of any opportunities which may be open to you to gain practical experience – and get feedback from others? Note them here.

3 Could any of *your* high priority development areas be seen as fairly low priority in your present job? If so, how could you revise them, to make them more 'employer friendly'?

4 Are there any informal ways you could arrange for your learning development?

5 Are there formal methods (e.g. appraisal/personal development plans (PDPs)) used to direct your progress within the company where you work? If so, how can you use these to best advantage?

6 What's the best way to find out about the opportunities available through your employer? Make a note of any valuable contact names and numbers here.

© Chris Sangster Development 2001

Format 4

ID Plan **Individual Planning System** ....**for a brilliant future.**
GOAT PLAN – Independent Development Routes

1   For specific development areas, what sources can you access (local enterprise agencies, learning accounts, investors in people, etc) to tap into affordable training? Note any good contacts you hear about.

2   Are there any people you know – or can network – who would help you get wider practical experience in an area you wish to develop? How could you make contact?

3   Which priority activities must you achieve, in order to meet both your short- and long-term development plans? How can you progress them?

4   What do you see as blocks, which may prevent you developing at the speed you would prefer? Once identified, is there a way round them – by getting help, perhaps?

5   Are there any self-study materials, books and other resources which may be available for you, through your local library, college, etc? Make a note of contact numbers and types of materials here.

6   Knowing the way(s) you like to learn and develop, what activities would really motivate you to progress further? How can you make them happen?

© Chris Sangster Development 2001

Format 5

ID Plan **Individual Planning System** ....for a brilliant future.
Am I going in the right direction?

1 What's my overall development plan for the next 6–12 months? What goal am I setting myself by the end of this chosen period of time?

2 If it involves a change in direction – how confident am I that the decision is correct? Are there any questions in my mind, still to be answered properly – if so, what?

3 Are there any people already doing what I want to achieve, whom I can talk to about the 'inside story'? Note their names and contact details here.

4 Do my nature, preferred ways of working, work/life preferences, etc match with the future 'me' that I am developing towards? If I still have doubts, how can I test myself – formally or informally?

5 If I think they are helpful, is it possible for me to complete any questionnaires or tests which might confirm whether I am suited for my planned direction? Who might I speak to, for details of these? Make contact notes here.

6 If my plans turn out to be too ambitious for my initial timescale, are there any intermediate milestones I can set, which will give me some idea of progress? Make a note of them here.

7 Do I still have any doubts? Make a note of them – and against each, write any actions which might clarify them.

© Chris Sangster Development 2001

Format 6

ID Plan **Individual Planning System** ....for a brilliant future.
Development Area Planning for ....*Development Area*
Format 2 cross-reference – Area ....*Overall priority rating.......*

1   Final outcome statement (write as action(s) you will be competent in achieving).

2   Possible methods of learning I would prefer (i.e. – not necessarily a course).

3   Steps and stages (milestones) along the way, which I can use to check that I'm progressing towards being competent.

   3.1
   3.2
   3.3
   3.4

4   Possible contacts, learning providers etc I can talk to, to get further information.

5   How can I get practical experience, to reinforce my learning? Note ideas here.

6   If I'm involved in recording my continuing professional development (CPD), how can I rewrite the statements in 3 above, so that they are statements of 'outcomes'?

7   Does this development area link directly with any of the others which I have identified as priorities? If so, are there any ideas for reinforcing these links and improving results?

© Chris Sangster Development 2001

Format 7

ID Plan Individual Planning System ....for a brilliant future.
Development Area Planning for ....Development Area
Format 2 cross-reference – Area..............Overall priority rating.......

Development Action Plan

1 What do I need to do to achieve it?

2 How do I want to do it?

3 What support have I identified?

4 What might prevent/slow me from doing it?

5 How can I get past this/these block(s)?

6 How do I start?

7 Who's my main contact?

8 What resources will I need?

9 How will I check and record my progress?

10 How will I know when I've achieved my goal/objective?

© Chris Sangster Development 2001

Format 8

ID Plan Individual Planning System ....for a brilliant future.
Development Area Planning for ....Development Area
Format 2 cross-reference – Area..............Overall priority rating.......

SHEEP PLAN – Linking with work

1   How do I apply this development area in my work?

2   Does the business give this a similar level of priority to mine? Y / N
     Comments

3   How do I sort out any differences of opinion on its priority and
     importance?

4   What level of support can I expect from the business?

5   What can I do to influence the situation?

6   How do I find out about any relevant future plans the business may
     have?

7   How can I use this knowledge to help my own development plan in this
     area?

8   From this view of the broader picture, what are some of my first
     milestones?

8.1

8.2

8.3

8.4

8.5

9   How do I best link these professional development ideas with the
     development plans which the company has for my job role?

© Chris Sangster Development 2001

Format 9

ID Plan Individual Planning System ....for a brilliant future.
Development Area Planning for ....Development Area
Format 2 cross-reference – Area..............Overall priority rating.......

GOAT PLAN – Taking the initiative

1 How can I get progress started for this development area?

2 How can I apply it within my own situation, to get further experience?

3 How can I make my objective more relevant, so that I can apply it more easily?

4 Where can I get support: finance, seminars, mentoring, informal coaching, etc?

5 How does this development area fit into my own 'bigger picture' for the future?

6 Is there any 'fine-tuning' which will make the whole plan work better?

7 From this view of the broader picture, what are some of my first milestones?

7.1
7.2
7.3
7.4
7.5

8 What techniques can I apply to help my motivation – and keep the whole thing driving forward?

© Chris Sangster Development 2001

Format 10

ID Plan Individual Planning System ....for a brilliant future.
Development Area Planning for ....Development Area
Format 2 cross-reference – Area..............Overall priority rating.......

Identifying the support

1   Firming up on detail in previous formats, what are the key issues (objectives, priorities, learning methods, etc) which I must address for this development area?

2   What possible support have I identified so far?

3   Which do I prefer and why?

4   Are there any other avenues I can try / people I can contact? Make notes.

5   Considering the 'best development option' I have at the moment, are there any gaps I will have to fill through extra learning and experience? Make notes.

6   Are there any other informal sources I can 'tap into', which will provide me with additional ideas, experience and practical reinforcement? Make notes.

7   From all this research, what is the best option open to me for this development area? Am I happy to go with this and will I need any additional support?

8   Will I have to find the funds to pay for any of this? If so, what sources can I use?

© Chris Sangster Development 2001

Format 11

ID Plan Individual Planning System ....for a brilliant future.
Development Area Planning for ....Development Area
Format 2 cross-reference – Area.............Overall priority rating.......

Checking on progress – informal

1   Referring to previous formats, am I reaching the milestones I had planned? Y/N If not, what can I do about it?

2   Do I need to review the way I'm doing things, to improve progress? How?

3   How are my planned timescales working out?

4   Are any of my intended solutions not really meeting my needs? If so, what can I do to refine these?

5   Have I encountered any blocks? How did I / will I get past them?

6   Am I getting better / more competent in this development area? Which things do I still need to focus on?

7   At the current stage of improving this development area, what do I have to do next?

8   What do I need to do, in order to finally reach my goal (outcome)?

9   What additional support do I need, in order to reach this goal?

© Chris Sangster Development 2001

Format 12

ID Plan **Individual Planning System ....for a brilliant future.**
Development Area Planning for ....Development Area
Format 2 cross-reference – Area..............Overall priority rating.......

Checking on progress – Optional formal
Continuing Professional Development – CPD
(This sheet can be used as a work-based CPD record for personnel purposes.)

1   Overall achieved objective statement.
    (I am capable of doing .... to .... standard.)

2   The outcomes of this development area are:
    (My related competencies are   )
2.1
2.2
2.3
2.4
2.5

3   The activities I carried out to achieve my learning outcomes included:

4   My activities relating to the development of others included:

5   The evidence supporting my competency achievement includes:

6   The relationship of this CPD Outcome with others achieved previously –
    and/or with others still to be attempted – is:

7   Signed ....Date ....Print name ....
    Detail confirmed by ....Print name ....
    Working relationship ....

© Chris Sangster Development 2001

Format 13

ID Plan Individual Planning System ....for a brilliant future.

Personal Development prompts

1   Am I satisfied with the way my life is developing overall? Y/N
    If – No – what can I do to change or refine my direction?

2   What can I do to improve my work/life balance?

3   How can I put something back into society?

4   What can I do to reduce the stress relating to my present work/life situation?

5   Are there any people I know/have heard of who might help me, if asked?

6   Do I spend enough time thinking about/focusing on the bigger picture of world activities and events? What are three areas of concern currently in the news?
    6.1
    6.2
    6.3

7   Am I aware of any people who need my help, in order to progress their development? If so, who – and what is the help they require, which I could provide?

8   Am I satisfied with my current level of spiritual awareness? If not, what would I like to do to improve it?

9   What is the first step I must take today, to progress my personal development?

© Chris Sangster Development 2001

Format 14

ID Plan Individual Planning System ....for a brilliant future.
Action Plan – Present & Future

Name ....Date ....Ref ....

Future Plan

1 Overall target

2 Sequence of milestones

Action	Proof of Achievement	Deadline

Present Plan

'Things to do' list

'Thing'	Priority	Done (✔)

© Chris Sangster Development 2001

Format 15

ID Plan Individual Planning System ....for a brilliant future.

Development Area Planning for..........................Development Area

Cross-reference – Area...........................Overall priority rating.........

Subject statement..

(Overwrite the following fields to meet your own particular needs.)

1 Statement Field
  Response Field

2 Statement Field
  Response Field

3 Statement Field
  Response Field

4 Statement Field
  Response Field

5 Statement Field
  Response Field

6 Statement Field
  Response Field

Open Response Field

Open Response Field

© Chris Sangster Development 2001